SOA for Profit

A Manager's Guide to Success with
Service Oriented Architecture

Martin van den Berg
Norbert Bieberstein
Erik van Ommeren

contributors
Per Björkegren, Sogeti Sweden
Jean-Marc Gaultier, Sogeti USA
Lon Holden, IBM Software Group USA
Manuel de Juan, Sogeti Spain
Tim Koomen, Sogeti Netherlands
Craig Mayer, Sogeti USA
Philippe Ravix, Sogeti France
Bruno Rizzi, Sogeti France
Gonzalo Rodriguez, Sogeti Spain
Guillaume Schott, Sogeti Belux
Gerard Smit, IBM Netherlands
Michiel Vroon, Sogeti Netherlands

2007
IBM and Sogeti

©2007   IBM and Sogeti

translation	George Hall
production	LINE UP boek en media bv, Groningen, the Netherlands
cover design	Jan Faber
cover photo	Shop ceiling (Paris) by Claudia Meyer (www.sxc.hu)
printing	Bariet, Ruinen, the Netherlands
binding	Abbringh, Groningen, the Netherlands
ISBN	978-90-75414-14-1

Acclaim for SOA for Profit

"Most current books about Service Oriented Architecture go to great lengths to explain the details of the nuts and bolts of web services and XML. Important as that is, those books ignore the central feature of service orientation, namely, that it is an approach to aligning business and IT that should cut costs and increase flexibility. This book focuses on this central feature of service orientation. It deals with important topics such as service maturity, practical steps to introduce SOA, service governance, and enterprise architecture for SOA. It does an excellent job in explaining to the manager in clear, non-technical terms what SOA can contribute to the business."

Prof Dr Roel Wieringa,
University of Twente

"A pragmatic and hands-on contribution to the evaluation of SOA as an architecture approach to create value for the business. The different views and complete set of IT considerations on SOA are supported by real and convincing examples. Gives a ready-to-use guide to adopt and implement SOA. Just an excellent source for anyone who wants to get to the next level of business and IT alignment based on SOA."

Henrik Jacobsson,
Lead IT Architect, Shell

"The question of what, when and how to communicate about SOA to business management and business analysts is a particularly difficult issue for IT architects. This book makes a useful contribution by communicating the essentials of service orientation in an approachable and non-technical manner that will assist a primarily business audience. "

David Sprott,
CBDI Forum

"The book 'SOA for Profit' shows managers and professional leaders capabilities and potentials of how using Service Oriented Architecture can contribute to organize and lead the enterprise in a more structured manner. Implementing SOA as an integral enterprise culture can increase corporate performance and profit."

Prof Thomas Obermeier, Vice Dean,
Fachhochschule der Deutschen Wirtschaft (FHDW) in Bergisch-Gladbach, Germany

"Everybody is talking about SOA nowadays and it is easy to brush it away by saying it is a hype. In reality it is a completely new way of working for IT internally and, most important, also an enabler for rapid business change, IT and business to get closer together. This book is the best I have read about this subject; it is an art to describe things in a good way for a wider audience and this book is a brilliant example of that."

Ingvar Persson,
IT Manager, Iggesund

"A comprehensive complete guide, thoroughly covering all relevant aspects based on experience and best practices available today. A sound starting point for any organization which believes SOA is not just an other hype and seeks a sustainable SOA implementation. Not 'SOA for dummies' but 'SOA for professionals'! Read it and you'll see."

Menno Bosman,
Information Manager, Fortis Insurance Netherlands

"There is a lot of fuss about SOA at the moment, but the question is whether we're talking hope or hype. This added interest could be because the supply side, software suppliers and consultants, is starting to wake up. This SOA book doesn't contain naïve statements about business processes; it doesn't contain middleware nitty-gritty or SOA fundamentalist techno-talk. Yes, it's actually about SOA. Fortunately it addresses the benefits of architecture and the significance of governance. It is well balanced, understandable and contains just the right emphasis.

A lot has been written about SOA. This book consolidates that information, while giving it proper perspective: how to achieve added business value using SOA. I highly recommend it for both managers and students. "

Jan Truijens,
Assistant Professor Business Studies and Information Management, Universiteit van Amsterdam

"The authors have packed a lot of real-world SOA experience into this book. Delivering sustainable business value from a SOA initiative requires much more than implementing a few pieces of technology, and this book offers invaluable practical advice about the organizational and cultural changes that you must anticipate and drive to succeed."

Neil Ward-Dutton,
Research Director, Macehitter Ward-Dutton

"After having published DYA, Sogeti has again succeeded in giving the architecture community a new approach, this time to SOA. Service Orientation is inevitable for modern network organizations, whilst Architecture makes SOA actively profitable. This book offers a broad description ranging from how to identify services in your business to the human factor. But most of all it provides practical insights about governance and down-to-earth do's and don'ts."

Arjan Bulthuis,
Dutch Ministry of Agriculture, Nature and Food Quality

"I have been reading the manuscript with increasing interest while travelling the globe. Conclusion: 'so it must have been worthwhile'. Though the table of contents seems a bit overdone at first, chapter titles such as 'Show me the money', 'Seven easy concepts, 'Govern or end up in a mess' and especially 'Ten great things to say to get fired', appealed to me at first sight and proved even more worth reading a second time. The focus on business, people and organization is very well chosen, and elaborated in much welcome detail without getting too technical (an advantage of this book!). A handy maturity measurement model and method is presented, whereas the concluding reference list is quite complete and even more important: up to date. If you want to know why I prefer the Bieberstein definition for SOA – you should read the book yourself. No regrets on my side..."

Dr Jan Peter de Valk,
ING

"This book serves as an introduction to SOA for both Business Managers and IT. It helps to explain and reiterate the concepts underpinning Service Oriented Architecture (SOA) which may already be familiar to experienced IT professionals. The discussion develops to show how, as standards have developed and reached industry-wide acceptance, the technology has also been maturing to the extent that tools, technologies, methodologies and best practice(s) are now available to mitigate risk for SOA adoption. This book helps to de-mystify SOA, supporting the theory with real-world experience to provide practical guidance on how to deliver successful SOA based projects."

Garry Gomersall,
SOA Evangelist and Business Executive, IBM Software Group

Foreword by IBM

Having been in this industry – and with IBM – for over 30 years, I've played an active role in the innovations that have shaped, challenged and taught us about the impact of technology in driving business. While many would point to the mainframe or eBusiness or open standards as inflection points that dramatically altered the way we function as departments and organizations, the most sweeping global shift in IT and business is clearly the advent of Service Oriented Architecture (SOA).

I realize the gravity of this statement and the shelf-life of this book and confidently reiterate that SOA has forever changed the way that business is conducted. Further, as business leaders and technologists, we have yet to fully exploit the positive and permanent effects that SOA has and will continue to have on companies of all sizes.

Game changer, innovation, preserving existing investments. I suppose you could reread analyst reports and trade magazine articles from years past that cite similar benefits of 'insert new technology here'. Don't confuse SOA with those past trends.

While many of those trends are still supporting business today, all too often they were categorized into buckets such as hardware, software or services and from there, subdivided once again so that each department within the larger IT team would know who was responsible for what once it was deployed in the infrastructure. It seemed to be a logical approach at the time. However, in a global economy that is increasingly more dependent on the symbiotic relationship between technology and business, we can no longer view the organization and the supporting infrastructure as separate pieces. This is where SOA proves most valuable. SOA spans the organization and delivers the most relevant information on demand to the appropriate business or IT user, regardless of the physical location of the employee, customer, or partner or even the source of the information.

There are many analysts, customers and CIOs who offer myriad anecdotes to support the claim that SOA represents the most powerful fusion of IT and business to advance the corporate agenda. More simply stated, let me share three tenets on why SOA is not the 'next big thing'. Rather, it is a strategy to more closely align technology with business goals. It is through this strategy that companies can realize greater productivity and bottom line results.

First, SOA is a way of doing business. Companies – and the technologies to support them – may come and go but SOA is a proven strategy for ensuring that all parts of the organization can freely and easily connect and communicate to maximize productivity while prioritizing the customers' needs. This, in turn, leads to my second point.

SOA fosters innovation. When employees, customers and partners can share information and ideas without being confined by the limitations of silos or proprietary applications, the result is innovative approaches to business. These innovations can range from streamlining business processes to global collaboration to creating breakthrough inventions.

Third, SOA uses and reuses existing knowledge, assets and investments. In some organizations, the term SOA is still mired in the trenches and leaves some to scratch their heads as they figure out what this new acronym really means. For those in the know, the upside is that SOA makes the most of existing sources of information and investments in technology and allows companies to reuse these without compromising the integrity of business functions. This ensures that the creation of the SOA is cost effective without requiring extensive training.

As you read through this book, you'll come to understand more fully the impact and the implications of SOA on organizations of all sizes. What's more, you'll realize that all that talk about 'the next big thing' – the time before SOA – was really just the warm up. So suit up, sit back and step up because SOA is here to stay.

Steve Mills
Senior Vice President and Group Executive
IBM Software Group

Foreword by Sogeti

One of the most attractive aspects of my job as CEO and Chairman of Sogeti is that I get to meet a lot of CxOs and have interesting discussions about how the role of IT is evolving in their increasingly challenging business reality. I am always amazed at the speed with which organizations have to react to changing circumstances. Usually IT is one of the crucial instruments to bring change about, but only too often IT also creates serious constraints on the ability to manoeuvre.

The book that you have in front of you is an important book. It is important because it is about the future of information technology and how IT will be able to support the business agility that is required for success. In a world where the only constant is change, enabling and supporting that change must become the key design factor for information systems.

Service Oriented Architecture is a philosophy and approach to create more agility from the start and, through systematic reuse, reduce the required effort to create and maintain functionality. However this is only part of the story. SOA stands for a state of mind that is of great influence on the collaboration between business management and IT to achieve the goal of greater business agility. It stands for the effort to automate a corporation or institution not along the lines it is structured, but rather along the lines the organization uses. Or, in other words, business agility can only be achieved when the focus shifts from functional, departmental stovepipes towards cross boundary business processes (eventually even crossing external boundaries). In a world where the value that an organization is adding becomes more and more transparent, a clear focus on the processes through which this value is added seems more than logical.

So, I am convinced that SOA is not only a tactical means of implementing information technology, it also stands for a much more strategic approach of supporting a redesign of organizations in a process-oriented fashion, delivering on the promise of business agility, inherently supported by information systems that not only enable but inspire business change.

Now, that being said, I am more than aware of the risks that such a claim brings. When IT people start to talk about restructuring the business to create business agility, most business managers can't help being just a little bit sceptical. And in a world dominated by tech booms and the burst that will inevitably follow, you can't really blame them.

That is where this book comes into play. Although the end goals for SOA remain quite ambitious, it is of the utmost importance to follow a realistic, step-by-step path towards those goals. Additionally, each step must deliver clear business benefit from the outset. The approach described in 'SOA for Profit' does exactly that. It offers a pragmatic, 'feet on the ground' approach to SOA where technical concepts always have to be expressed in business value and where business agility is created through new forms of collaboration between business and IT. The book offers the necessary inspiration to justify investment in this new architecture while at the same time offering guidance to make sure the expected business value is created. In that sense it is a journey whose destination is clear, but whose route is not. The promise is business agility and a hugely improved relation between business and IT. However there are many perils along the road that have to be overcome. To start out on this journey a healthy dose of pragmatism is as important as a clear sense of direction. I believe the main contribution of this book is that it helps develop the 'SOA Leadership' that really is crucial in getting profit from Service Oriented Architecture.

Luc-François Salvador
Chairman and Chief Executive Officer
Sogeti

Preface

IBM and Sogeti are both companies with an excellent pedigree. One of the fields in which they closely collaborate is Service Oriented Architecture. The idea of writing a book with a joint vision on this topic arose in the summer of 2006. Now, less than a year later, the book has appeared. This is a splendid achievement when one considers that an international team from two different companies had to realize the task, that most people scarcely knew one another, and that six different languages were spoken. It is with fitting pride that we can now present SOA for Profit.

This book is a guide for managers and architects who are responsible or are intensely involved in the implementation of SOA within their organizations. We have opted to direct this book to them in particular. This means that we have not covered technical and technological aspects. Although these may be extremely interesting in themselves, they are not of primary importance in the implementation of SOA in an organization. We have placed the emphasis on the essential factors that need to be addressed: governance, architecture, and the development of a broad vision on SOA.

A great many people have made a contribution to the substance of this book. First of all, these were the authors who supplied the various chapters. The authors from IBM were Norbert Bieberstein and Gerard Smit, and from Sogeti, Martin van den Berg, Per Björkegren, Tim Koomen, Craig Mayer, Erik van Ommeren, Bruno Rizzi, and Michiel Vroon.

In addition, various contributors have assisted in supplying best practices and other relevant information. Our gratitude in this domain goes to Manuel de Juan, Jean-Marc Gaultier, Lon Holden, Philippe Ravix, Gonzalo Rodriquez, and Guillaume Schott.

We also wish to thank Piet Jan Baarda, Jan Hoogervorst, Ruud Steeghs, and Marlies van Steenbergen for proofreading the manuscript.

Special thanks must be extended to René Speelman for leading the workshops that helped define the structure and message of the book.

We have worked on this book with the utmost pleasure, and we hope that you will read it with an equal degree of enjoyment. We wish you much success in applying the insights contained in this book when implementing SOA in your organization. We would be interested to hear your experiences. Please email them to soa@sogeti.nl.

March 2007
Martin van den Berg
Norbert Bieberstein
Erik van Ommeren

Table of contents

1 The journey begins

Even the longest journey begins with a single step. But what is this first step you take in order to solve the greatest problems currently plaguing organizations that use IT? How can you prevent ever increasing maintenance costs paralysing an organization? How can you reach a situation in which your time-to-market is fast enough to have a chance of survival in today's internet world? How can you find your way out of the current predicament of silos, spaghetti, and rigid IT?

Service Oriented Architecture (SOA) is a next step on the path to maturity of IT as a professional discipline and a next step in the way business can make use of IT. SOA is an architectural style in which systems are divided according to simple concepts that, when they are combined, guarantee extremely flexible and controllable IT. The basic concept is that all IT is composed of services: elementary components that remain relatively stable regardless of the changes within the organization. These services can then be used to quickly realize new products and services. SOA also addresses the threat of getting deadlocked as a result of continuously increasing management and maintenance costs; SOA, and the associated reuse of services, makes IT simpler and cheaper to maintain. Above all, Service Oriented Architecture is not only a development within the domain of IT, it also has a far reaching impact on the organization that makes use of this IT. Indeed, the organizational aspect is of decisive importance.

Ensuring coherence when various changes are carried out makes the implementation of SOA no easy task. A change in your IT will be necessary, and also the cooperation between your business and IT will change. And prior to setting out on your journey, you will have to deliberate on your business objectives, and consider whether or not it is realistic to expect to reach these goals by means of SOA. Whatever the case, SOA is not an aim in itself, it is not a ready-made technology, it is no quick fix. SOA is architecture, with all the corresponding properties: it requires discipline and patience to implement it, step by step.

If you decide to implement SOA, it is impossible to tackle everything at once. You will have to establish priorities and make choices. Then you can plan the first stage. This first stage consists mainly of business projects that bring direct added value, as well as projects that are geared to preparing various aspects of your organization for dealing effectively with SOA.

Service Oriented Architecture is here to stay. Just as dispensing with mathematics will never be logical, dispensing with the concepts behind Service Oriented Architecture will never be prudent. And it is here that SOA distinguishes itself *in nature* from other hypes: it is not a hype, it is a growth spurt. And, as such, the journey towards SOA has become more attractive: are you in for growth?

1.1 Goal

SOA for Profit offers you a guide to plan your route toward SOA and arrive at your destination successfully. You are furnished with lines of approach, models and tips so that you can formulate a vision of SOA, can determine where you are, and can draw up a roadmap for the route to SOA.

This book enables you to:
* Assess the added value of SOA for your organization.
* Understand the concepts behind SOA.
* Survey the consequences of implementing SOA.
* Identify the right steps to implement SOA in your organization.

1.2 Target audience

This book has been specially written for those who are responsible for the implementation of SOA within their organization. In particular CIOs, IT managers, business managers, information managers, process managers, change managers, project managers, and enterprise architects can obtain great benefit from this book.

In addition, this book is useful for people who are regularly involved in SOA projects in their organization, such as product managers, business architects, IT architects, process designers, business analysts, information analysts, software engineers and testers.

1.3 Structure

The topic of Service Oriented Architecture is elaborated increasingly concretely and practically in the course of the book. The outline moves from concept and vision to concrete projects, as well as dealing with the pitfalls that ought to be avoided.

In Chapter 2, the book begins with the motivation behind SOA. Why are we talking about it and what makes it so interesting? This chapter provides the rational basis for the rest of the book. It describes examples of organizations that have benefited from the implementation of SOA.

Chapter 3 discusses the essence of SOA in the form of seven easy concepts, leading into the most important precondition for the successful application of SOA: Governance. The implementation of SOA without any form of Governance will irrevocably lead to chaos. Chapter 4 demonstrates that Enterprise Governance and Enterprise Architecture are indispensable, and you are offered tips to install these competencies within your organization.

Another essential precondition in the implementation of SOA is to start with the business. When services are designed, the business is taken as the starting point. This can only be done by applying a certain type of abstraction, also referred to as 'business modeling'. In this modeling, use may be made of existing industry models. These designs are covered in Chapter 5. Thinking in terms of services need not be restricted to IT systems. An organization itself can be defined in terms of services, which brings the prospect of a 'service oriented enterprise'. Chapter 6 deals with this further perspective on SOA.

Chapter 7 discusses the impact of SOA on people in an organization. After all, SOA entails a different way of working when changes to the business and IT are implemented.

Chapters 3 to 7 largely cover the consequences and preconditions of implementing SOA. SOA has a major impact, and any implementation entails major consequences. Chapter 8 gathers these consequences and puts them into perspective in a SOA Maturity Model. This model enables you to determine just how mature your organization is in the field of SOA, and which improvement measures you can take to reach the desired level of ambition.

Implementing SOA takes place mostly within regular business projects. These are projects in which the business invests in putting a new product on the market, for example, or improving its processes. Chapter 9 covers the identification of business projects for the application of SOA. The so-called 'Entry Points' give support to this process.

With SOA, the organization is furnished with a very widespread set of components (the services) that are as autonomous as possible, and are used at various places. To complete the SOA journey successfully, it is essential to test adequately the services and the business processes in which these services are used. This is the topic of Chapter 10.

The implementation of SOA brings an avalanche of consequences. Organizations that were pioneers in this field encountered pitfalls that you can better avoid. Chapter 11 summarizes the ten most important pitfalls.

In conclusion, Chapter 12 contains a summary, and speculates on the future of SOA.

More detailed information on the SOA Maturity Model has been included in Appendix 1.

SOA for Profit is not a technical discourse. The challenge of SOA implementation lies to a greater extent in preparing the organization in such a way that the chance of success is enhanced and the promises given by SOA – more flexibility and lower costs – are indeed redeemed.

The book contains various examples from real life. These examples have been placed in frames so that they can be easily recognized.

2 Show me the money

2.1 Introduction

Is the IT within your organization always the critical point when the business is ready to innovate? Have you been busy for years trying to integrate processes and systems after a merger or takeover? Are you missing market opportunities because you are too late in introducing new products? Have IT and business in your organization great difficulty in understanding one another? Are the costs of management and maintenance of IT in your organization steadily increasing?

If these questions have evoked a feeling of recognition, you should certainly read on. SOA will enable you to tackle these problems. SOA is a way of arranging business and IT in such a manner that your organization becomes considerably more flexible and efficient.

In 2000, a large financial service company observed that its cost/income ratio – an efficiency indicator for banks – was 70.8 per cent. This meant that it was one of the poorest performers in the sector. The rather high cost figure was due to fragmented, and thus inefficient, operation and IT, representing a bottleneck in the organization's objective of developing into a world-class financial operator. Things had to change and change drastically. Costs and risks had to be cut, productivity increased, and the IT had to be standardized and consolidated in order to arrive at an operation and IT that enabled the business instead of restricting it. To achieve these aims, an architecture fully based on SOA was designed and implemented in the company. This brought success. In 2006, the cost/income ratio has been reduced to 62.3 per cent. Partly due to SOA, this organization has managed to lower costs, improve flexibility, and accelerate business development, all of which have confirmed the promises of SOA.

Any business manager will ask: 'SOA, it's a nice story, but can I make money with it?'. This chapter illustrates how SOA can lead to added value. You will gain insight into why organizations opt for SOA and what this can achieve. In addition, you are given indications of what SOA can mean in your own situation. This chapter will show you the money.

2.2 Why SOA?

Change is the only constant factor in organizations. External pressure is the main cause of organizations having to continually adapt. The drivers of change include legislation and regulations, opportunities on the market, technological possibilities, fulfilment of compliance criteria, the growing market in the Far East, the potential for outsourcing, the pressure to restrict costs, etc. The speed with which organizations can anticipate these factors determines their competitive capability. Speed and flexibility are the distinguishing aspects here.

However, realizing speed and flexibility is not an easy task. Organizations have processes and systems that have become so complex and interwoven that it is a devil of a job trying to adjust them. A prime example of this is a retailer who was very successful. The number of branches increased so rapidly that the establishment code had to be expanded. The impact analysis alone, which was necessary to find out which systems had to be adapted, required no fewer than 40,000 hours.

Another example is that of a government organization whose IT productivity declined as the result of the increasing complexity of the IT systems. The actual adjustment of the systems was quite limited, but the time required for prior analysis and tests continued to increase.

SOA offers the possibility to break this trend. With the proper application of SOA principles in the structuring of processes and systems, and the appropriate implementation of SOA-based technology, an organization irrefutably improves its speed and flexibility. SOA not only disengages processes from systems but also disconnects systems from one another. Organizations traditionally have to cope with large, complex, monolithic systems that not only offer a jungle of functionality but also prescribe how the business process should be executed. If this process has to be adapted, the system has to be adjusted and this entails a great deal of investigative and test work. With SOA, the functionality is cut up into smaller units, such as 'show new customer', for example. This kind of small unit is made available as a service, an automated business task, to all business processes in which the new customer is presented. If the process has to be adjusted, this can be done much more rapidly and simply because we do not need to plod through the entire system. Furthermore, a service can be reused in various processes, which can lead to substantial cost savings because we use what we already have instead of buying something new, which in turn means there is less software to maintain and support.

It can be rightly claimed that SOA represents a big step forward: it is the next step in the IT maturing process. SOA now offers IT the right approach to address business in a language that it can comprehend. After all, the required functionalities can be defined in terms of services. The way in which these functionalities are subsequently supplied by IT is not particularly interesting to the business. The 'what' is completely separated from the 'how'.

The implementation of SOA is not a goal in itself. SOA is a means to make an organization more flexible and cost effective. Thus, if these business-related aims play a role in your organization, it is important to consider SOA. In the longer term, we expect that SOA will develop into the *de facto* architectural style for the layout of business and IT. Large suppliers of business applications, such as SAP, Microsoft and Oracle are investing hundreds of millions in order to be able to offer their applications as services. In addition, software and hardware suppliers such as IBM and HP are making gigantic investments in order to make their products SOA-compatible. Even if SOA is perhaps not opportune for you at this moment, you will have to deal with it sooner or later. That is why it is important to read on and examine what SOA can mean for your organization.

2.3 Why do organizations choose SOA?

There are various reasons why organizations choose SOA. To some, it is a logical consequence of the chosen business strategy, whereas to others, it is not a choice but rather a question of survival.

The example in the Introduction deals with an organization that has chosen SOA in order to realize its ambition of becoming a world-class financial provider. We will now present three cases that demonstrate various reasons why organizations choose SOA:
1. Strategic considerations, because the chain of which the organization is part is about to alter.
2. A matter of necessity; SOA is the only alternative in order to survive.
3. A combination of obsolete technology and changing demands from the business.

The first example covers an organization that regards SOA as a strategic choice in connection with its changing role in European money transfer activities.

Automated Clearing House

One of the largest and most advanced Automated Clearing Houses in Europe has opted for SOA as a principle for structuring business and IT. The reasons to choose SOA are the increasing internationalization in the field of money transfer in Europe and the consequent positioning of this organization as a full-service provider of giral and card-related processing, switching, clearing, and settlement. This choice leads to increased cooperation in the chain and also to possible mergers. This organization has opted for SOA from the point of view of business agility and cost management. A stringent disconnection of the IT layers themselves, as shown in Figure 2.1, along with an integrated architectonic link with the organizational processes, forms a central feature of SOA. This should lead to the discontinuation or avoidance of undesired connections and overlaps in the processes. It is not limited to the organization itself but also extends to possible merger groups, customers, and other parties in the chain. In this, SOA is not restricted to the IT domain, but starts with the services that the organization supplies to the market and extends to the services that the infrastructural domain supplies to enable the running of applications. The result must eventually be a better and more dynamic alignment of business and IT.

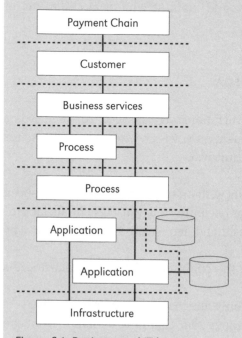

Figure 2.1 Business and IT layers

However, there are also organizations that choose SOA because there are no further alternatives. They must apply SOA in order to survive. It is a question of 'do or die'. Processes and systems have become so complex that the organization threatens to be snowed under. The second example illustrates this.

Telecommunication company

What makes a well-established telco company, with more than 8 million clients, move to SOA for all its business processes regarding its prepaid business line? All of them, at the same time, in a huge two-year, 12m€ project...

What caused this mess? Let's describe the initial scenario that forced such drastic decision.

Low quality developments

If there is a common trait in business models with regard to cellular and mobile service providers, it is fast and aggressive time-to-market values. This leads to the necessity to have very short development life cycles that challenge the skills and endurance of development teams. Milestones and deadlines can never be missed if you want to be the first to deliver a new service.

However, this need for speed often has adverse consequences if it's not properly managed. This was the case with this telco. Although it did have a Software Quality Department that provided development procedures and best practices, the analysis and design phases within development projects were usually dismissed as 'non-productive' steps due to lack of time, so everyone strove to deliver something that worked as soon as possible, without sufficient attention being paid to quality. This led to the following scenarios:

- Software modules (online forms, batch jobs, transactions...) evolved into such obscure and messy spawns that no one had enough time to fully explore which things had already been done and how. No good old Analysis and Design phases were implemented. Every new development just contributed to making the whole mess bigger.
- New service developments were hardly aligned with other existing ones. There was no way anyone would invest precious time in trying to explore the best way to fit the product into the whole portfolio.
- There was a lack of information about the common modules available to different development teams, as documentation had not been a critical step. There was no structure covering reuse.

High expenses in production environment maintenance

As a direct consequence of low quality development, there were defects in the software delivered, even in the production environment. In many cases, these defects were not easy to solve as they were embedded in non-structured, rather chaotic software modules. As a consequence, the budget and resources needed to support these critical environments – so close to the end user – increased so substantially every year that the situation threatened to undermine the whole company performance.

Architecture not adapting enough to market changes

Our telco organization was very focused on its CRM system. This was based on a major strategic decision that had been taken years previously, when Call Centers were the main entry point of every single interaction with the clients: new services demands, changes of existing ones, client information alterations, etc. Thus, the IT architecture had been highly influenced by this business decision: nearly all the business process developments implemented were hosted within their CRM, and the other systems were slaves to this master.

Figure 2.2 depicts that business logic was hosted within the CRM system, changes were updated in the CRM system database and then other systems were notified of these changes.

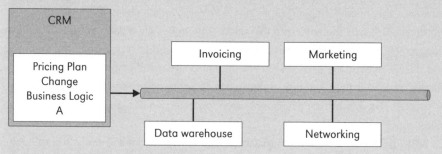

Figure 2.2 Pricing Plan Change

Further technological improvements allowed other channels to become at least as relevant as Call Centers (classical CRM). So they welcomed interactive portals, Short Message Services (SMS), Interactive Voice Response (IVR) systems, and many other facilities. All these channels had to provide flexibility to the user, so that a client had different choices to perform the same action. Then, what happened to the business logic?

Figure 2.3 demonstrates that the Business logic of Pricing Plan Change was so embedded in the CRM implementation that it was impossible for other new channels to reuse it. Therefore, every channel built its own solution to the same business process.

It is easy to imagine the kind of problem that this type of architectural solution generated. Whenever a change in this process was required, it had to be developed in four different environments! There were also different maintenance teams for these systems, so the patches applied to solve defects diverged as well. Within a few months, this business process, which was meant to provide the same functionality regardless of the channel used, evolved to provide different features that solved the same problems in different ways. The architecture of this telco lacked the flexibility to adapt as fast as the market required, and therefore the choice for SOA was more than obvious.

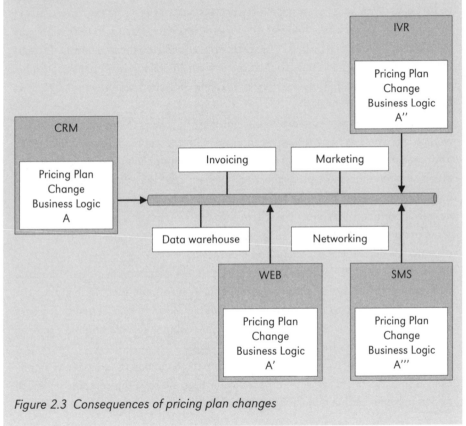

Figure 2.3 Consequences of pricing plan changes

The third and last example is that of an organization that opted for SOA due to the combination of obsolete technology and changing demands from the business.

Starwood Hotels

In 2001, Starwood Hotels realized that Service Oriented Architecture was its future [CIO Insight 2006]. The international hotel chain, which includes brands such as the St. Regis Hotels, Sheraton, Westin's and the W Hotels, saw that its awkward and costly old system was limiting the company's ability to accommodate rapidly growing distribution channels such as Internet. It was too difficult to add capabilities to the CRM system, do proper searching to find properties – in short, many of the things a modern IT environment needs.

Starwood's current systems were also having difficulty handling the rapidly increasing traffic on its Web sites, what hospitality professionals refer to as the 'look-to-book' ratio. In the old days of the Internet, the look-to-book ratio was 50 to 1. Now it's 300 to 1. So they needed an IT environment that could handle all those requests. To keep the legacy system would have required a multi-million dollar investment in upgrades and technical support. This was very costly, and Starwood didn't want to be held down.

So Starwood began the long process of moving its systems to an open SOA framework. It was the best way to map technology with their various brands. Instead of having each of Starwood's hotel chains build its own applications, SOA allows the brands to share the same programs and features – but they can be customized for each hotel's specific look and feel. Sheraton's search function, for example, may deliver information differently than, say, that of the W Hotels, even though it's the same program. That way Starwood benefits from using all the same tools that can be activated by different applications and interfaces.

Because SOA loosens dependencies, meaning that services can be activated across different operating systems and environments, it also generates flexibility for the company to create new tools. Starwood has put in place an application that tracks guest requests and complaints, for example. The company also created a program that stores and tracks frequent guests' preferences.

But it didn't happen overnight. After five years, the company is finally ready to officially dismantle its old system – an endeavour that will save the company as much as $20 million a year in maintenance costs.

The three examples discussed demonstrate that there are diverse reasons why organizations opt for SOA. These reasons may vary from strategic considerations, as in the first example, in which the chain, of which the organization is a component, is about to alter, to a matter of necessity as in the second example. In the third example, the limits of the current system have been reached.

2.4 **What's in it for me?**

The question as to what SOA can offer you is fully dependent on your specific situation and particularly the business problems and challenges. A good way of ascertaining whether or not SOA is suitable for your situation is to formulate a business vision on SOA. This business vision helps make clear what the advantages and the consequences of SOA can be for an organization. The business vision can help determine whether or not SOA should be implemented and, if so, where to begin. To sketch a picture of the advantages that can be obtained with SOA, we shall make use of a study that IBM performed on 35 SOA implementations in 5 different industrial sectors [IBM Global Business Services 2006b]. This research indicated that improving the business flexibility is the greatest benefit of implementing SOA, with cost reduction as a good second. Table 2.1 displays the advantages of implementing SOA, in order of importance.

Improved flexibility	Improved ability to change Increased asset reuse Decreased system integration time Decreased Time To Market (TTM)
Cost reduction	Lower system integration costs Lower development and system maintenance costs Lower business and IT operational costs
Risk reduction	Improved availability and reliability Improved flexibility of the organization Improved security
Increased revenue	Realization of new revenue streams Increased current revenue streams Maintenance of current revenue streams
New product development	Creation of new services by using current and/or new systems Faster creation and delivery of new products
Compliance	Improved transparency Improved accuracy and vigilance

Table 2.1 Observed advantages from SOA projects

The IBM study further indicated that there were various reasons to implement SOA. These reasons are listed in Table 2.2 and seem to be partly related to frustration and partly to opportunities on the market, as was also the conclusion with regard to the three examples in the previous section.

Necessity of technology change	Old/inappropriate legacy environments Insufficient capacity, low reliability Rigid systems that are resistant to change
Possibility of collaboration	Necessity of exchanging information and services with partners, suppliers, distributors, and customers
Competitive pressure	Competitor anticipates faster and more flexible solutions Faster delivery of products and services Improved customer services (customer services/customer satisfaction)
Legislation	Compliance/legal mandates from government and/or the business itself
Supplier/distributor requirements	Request for improved connectivity Decreased ownership of point-to-point solutions
New markets	Use new and current services to open new channels

Table 2.2 Incentives for SOA projects

Thus, various benefits and reasons can be distinguished in real-life practice. These benefits and reasons for choosing SOA are elements that make up part of the business vision as outlined in Figure 2.4.

The business vision consists of five elements: reason, benefits, definition, consequences, and implementation.

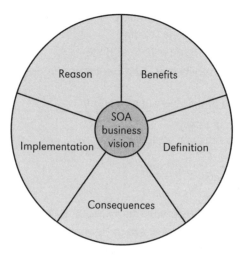

Figure 2.4 SOA business vision elements

Reason

The decision to embark on SOA doesn't come out of thin air. There has to be a reason. The motivation can come from many different sources both inside and outside the organization. An example of an internal driver is the application landscape that is completely clogged and unable to handle a single additional modification, or an organization that wants to move from product focus to process focus. An external driver is, for example, a standard package supplier who has incorporated services into the latest version of his tool, or a partner who provides web services rather than exchanging data using EDI messages. The reason usually has to do with pain or an urgent need. Pain is internal to the organization and must be resolved, and, with an eye toward the future, be prevented. An urgent need is almost always externally triggered and often has to be handled without business case discussion.

Benefits

Determining the SOA benefits is the next step in defining the business vision. The temptation is to accept the first list one comes across. Please try to resist this. It is important to define the advantages as specifically as possible for the particular organization. That means that there has to be a connection between the goals of an organization and the SOA possibilities. We developed two questionnaires to assist in revealing that connection.

Are you a business manager, then read this!

Imagine you are a business manager and are visited by an IT manager who launches into a sermon about SOA. What can you as a business manager do? The solution: ask questions! Take the bull by the horns and ask the IT manager questions.

Questions to help you to form an opinion:
- How can IT contribute to our business goals?
- What could SOA contribute to our business?
- Could SOA also be an enabler for our organization?
- Which areas are most likely to benefit from SOA?
- What are the risks and consequences of introducing SOA?

Specific questions for the business to ask IT:
- What is IT's contribution in achieving my business objectives?
- What services can IT offer to me (as a business) considering that we, as a company, also deliver services to our clients in the market?

- Please explain in 5 minutes what SOA means to our company and what it means to me in particular?
- SOA sounds like something techy, why is it important to me?
- Please provide me with some scenarios how IT can help me shorten our time-to-market for new products?
- Please provide some scenarios showing how IT can help me cut costs in the short as well as the long term?
- Please provide some scenario's showing how IT can help me improve the agility and flexibility of our organization?
- Is SOA the next IT industry hype, or is it something sustainable, and why?
- What do I need to do when deploying SOA in our organization? How many years does it take and what will it cost?
- Are we ready for SOA? When would we be ready?
- Does it fit into our culture?
- What are the preconditions for successful deployment of SOA in our organization?
- What are the implementation risks?
- Are there any quick wins?
- What about our competitors? Are they deploying SOA? Why? What are their experiences?
- What are the benefits to me and our customers?
- What will happen if we decide not to invest?

The answers to these questions should light a fire under the IT department and get them to think with you instead of seeing SOA as a goal in itself.

Are you an IT manager, then read this!
Imagine that you, as an IT manager, want to arouse the interest of the business manager in SOA. What should you do? You shouldn't be selling SOA in itself, but assesss exactly where SOA brings added value to the business. Once again what you need to do is ask questions!

Questions that can help you assess:
- Can SOA also be an enabler in our organization?
- What are the drivers for SOA?
- Where do I start?
- When do I start?
- What are the risks and consequences?

Questions for IT to ask the business:

- What are our business objectives, in the short and long term?
- What is our long-term mission and vision?
- How are we performing compared to our competitors? In which areas do we perform better? In which areas do we perform worse?
- What are our company strengths and weaknesses?
- What are our company opportunities and threats?
- Are there any plans for business process improvement? In which areas? What are the objectives?
- Are there any plans for mergers and acquisitions?
- Are there any plans to improve supply chain management? What are the objectives?
- Are there any plans for cost cutting? In which areas? What are the objectives?
- Are there any plans for introducing new products or services, or to enter new markets?
- Are there any compliance initiatives within our organization? What are the objectives?
- Is synergy on the agenda of the board? If so, in which areas do you think we can achieve synergy?
- How satisfied are you with IT? In which areas are you completely dissatisfied? In which areas are you completely satisfied?
- Do you think IT is an inhibitor to change in our organization? If so, to what extent does it inhibit? Please illustrate with some concrete examples.
- What is your opinion of defining requirements to IT in terms of services and service levels that you want IT to deliver?
- Do you think the concept of shared service centers is suitable for our organization? Why do you think that?
- As in most companies, we tend to reinvent the wheel. What possibilities do you see for reusing information, processes, or whatever?
- What do you expect from IT in general?
- Please try to describe your ideal scenario of how Business and IT should collaborate?
- What is your worst-ever experience with IT?
- What is your best-ever experience with IT?
- What is your number one requirement of IT?
- Have you ever heard about SOA? If so, what do you think about it? Do you see benefits for our organization?
- In the next few years, what will be the most important capability for our organization? Why?

Determining the SOA benefits is not intended as a writing process where an architect or consultant comes up with an enthralling document while sitting behind his desk, but is rather an awareness process that uses workshops to associate the business goals with the possibilities of SOA. This process can be described as a strategic dialogue between business and IT. A strategic dialogue is a continuous process through which the business goals are established and finally elaborated into concrete project proposals by means of business cases. The business goals are discussed in a dialogue between business and IT. The deliverable part of a strategic dialogue regarding SOA is a list of benefits tailored to the specific organization with the necessary justification and with a broad understanding of, and commitment to, the organization.

 Definition
The third element of a SOA business vision, the 'what', is just as important as the 'why' (the benefits). Using a SOA definition, a company-specific definition of SOA can be documented and the required aspects identified.

Just as with themes such as Enterprise Architecture and IT Governance, there is a plethora of definitions of the term 'Service Oriented Architecture'. It doesn't matter which one is correct, but rather which is the most appropriate for your organization. A judgement needs to be made as to the objectives of the SOA and which definition is most appropriate. Figure 2.5 (see page 35) presents a number of SOA definitions.

 Consequences
In addition to benefits, there are also a number of consequences associated with the selection of a SOA. It is important to have a broad overview of these consequences early in the decision-making process, as these will largely determine the success and the investment level within a company.

In real life, each consequence of a SOA is an investment. And, as with every change, there are associated costs. Common consequences of a SOA implementation are:
* There will need to be a greater emphasis on process focused effort.
* The governance and architectural processes change.
* The business development process changes.
* The IT development process changes.
* The administration and maintenance processes change.

- IT personnel will require retraining.
- Business personnel will require retraining.
- New tooling will be required.

We shall discuss these implementation consequences in greater detail later. When defining the business vision it is important to identify and detail all the relevant consequences in order to make an informed decision on whether the business can and will bear them.

Gartner:	**CBDI:**	**W3C:**	**Bieberstein et al:**
Service Oriented Architecture (SOA) is a client/server software design approach in which an application consists of software services and software service consumers (also known as clients or service requesters)	The policies, practices, frameworks that enable application functionality to be provided and consumed as sets of services published at a granularity relevant to the service consumer. Services can be invoked, published and discovered, and are abstracted away from the implementation using a single, standards-based form of interface.	A set of components which can be invoked, and whose interface descriptions can be published and discovered	A framework for integrating business processess and supporting IT infrastructure as secure, standardized components – services – that can be reused and combined to address changing business priorities

Figure 2.5 Definitions of a SOA

Implementation

The fifth and final business vision element is implementation. The implementation of SOA is discussed in general terms. This implementation is not a linear process, as there can be multiple implementations running concurrently. What is important in this chapter is that the structures for financing, initiation, implementation and management are outlined. In order to have a solid idea of what SOA can offer, a number of application examples have to be included in the implementation chapter.

As mentioned earlier, the definition of a business vision is a process. The awareness and acceptance of SOA within a company can be greatly enhanced by including the relevant stakeholders, such as process managers, IT managers, administrators and architects, in this process. A workshop on methodology is eminently suited to generating a business vision. Different people from different disciplines can be brought together to work towards a common goal.

Defining a business vision is an activity that can best be facilitated by people with consulting expertise who are capable of relating the SOA concepts to the business challenges of the organization.

Besides the previously mentioned benefits, a business vision is an excellent means of announcing the SOA message within your organization at numerous communication moments.

Perhaps you may be wondering why no business case is made for SOA. There are a number of reasons why we advise against this. The most important of these is that SOA should not become an aim in itself. SOA is an architecture style that is extremely suitable for an organization that needs to cope with many changes. We do advise making business cases for these changes, such as the improvement of processes or the introduction of a new product to the market. Another reason for not making a business case for SOA is the fact that it is impossible to calculate the effects of SOA on the profitability of an organization. There are many factors that influence profitability, and it is impossible to separate the SOA effect. The third and final reason is that the implementation of SOA represents a journey. At the start of the journey, you know where you want to go but the exact route is not yet apparent. It is only after the first stage has been completed that you have a better sight of the second stage. In short, it is impossible to plot out a clear path for the SOA in advance. SOA is not a revolution, there is no big bang approach to implementing SOA. SOA is more of an evolution: the implementation of SOA can be performed step by step, with each step furnishing added value.

In order to be certain of where you wish to go with SOA, we advise you to formulate a business vision on SOA. This will not only help in clarifying your objectives but also provide an indication of whether or not you should undertake this journey and, if so, what you need to take with you. Subsequently, you can plan the first SOA stage in relation to a concrete business problem. You can formulate a business case for this, and it will also force you to implement SOA where the urgency is the greatest.

2.5 When is SOA not for me?

SOA is inevitable in the long run. An increasing number of major suppliers and end-user organizations are applying SOA. This means that more and more software and hardware is being based on SOA, that an increasing amount of functionalities are being made available as services, and that a growing number of chains and co-operative endeavours are being structured in a service-based manner. Thus, sooner or later, there will be no escape.

It remains to be seen whether you should anticipate SOA or should simply wait until SOA overtakes you. SOA is particularly suitable for an organization with heterogeneous IT that has to cope with many changes. All Fortune 500 organizations come into this category. Organizations that are highly dependent on IT, such as banks, insurance companies, and telcos, are also part of this group. These organizations are advised to conduct a strategic dialogue on SOA and to record it in a business vision on SOA.

At the other end of the spectrum, there are organizations with homogeneous IT that are undergoing relatively few changes. What these organizations have to gain by taking the initiative and implementing SOA remains a moot point. For example, a small industrial enterprise almost exclusively operating with SAP will probably benefit more from the SAP strategy.

It is interesting to note that there may be company departments or functions within a single organization that make completely different demands on the IT, and therefore have an impact on the possible choice of SOA. In general, SOA is less suitable when there is mention of homogeneous IT, when real-time performance is extremely important, and when things do not change very substantially.

2.6 Summary

It should be clear that the implementation of SOA can be financially rewarding for an organization. Money can be made by means of a more efficient use of IT and a more flexible business that can innovate and improve more rapidly. In real-life practice, SOA has often redeemed its promise whether it is because of strategic considerations or a matter of necessity.

It is important to realize that SOA is not an aim in itself. It is a means to make an organization more flexible and cost effective. The formulation of a business vision on SOA is therefore an essential first step in the exploration of the possibilities of SOA for your organization. This kind of business vision consists of five elements – reason, benefits, definition, consequences, and implementation – and is a powerful tool in assisting you to make money with SOA.

3 The essence of SOA in seven easy concepts

3.1 Introduction

SOA is easy. The basic concepts of SOA are easy to explain, even to someone who is unfamiliar with IT. To a large extent, SOA is common sense, clever thinking, and perhaps ... wishful thinking. Service Oriented Architecture in a greenfield world is the most logical and practical way of doing IT. Sadly, there's very little greenfield in the world of IT. Nevertheless, to derive benefits, or even to be able to decide if there are possible benefits for your company, a clear picture of SOA is important.

In this chapter we shall talk about the perception of SOA and explain what SOA is, in terms that are as old as IT itself, or even older.

While the concepts themselves may be easy, changing the way your organization works with IT will take time: the transition to Service Oriented Architecture will be gradual but it will surely have a major impact on IT and business.

3.2 Perception of SOA

One of the greatest challenges companies face when adopting SOA is gathering enough knowledge on the subject to discern the real value, the real challenges, and the most profitable steps to take. Gathering knowledge turns out to be a challenge on its own. Service Oriented Architecture wasn't invented by one company. There's no standards body that has the authority to declare 'what SOA is'. There is little or no consensus on what makes any particular architecture fit the term 'Service Oriented Architecture'. Many organizations in the IT arena have developed their own vision on SOA, nicely fitting their own product lines or services. Even the great visionaries in the field, like Gartner, Forrester or, experts on SOA, the CBDI forum, all use different models and terminology. All this clouds the water significantly, adding to the problem instead of creating a solution.

At the same time, the perception that IT professionals have of SOA is much broader than simply 'having an architecture based on services'. SOA has now become a synonym for 'doing IT correctly' in the broadest interpretation one can think of. SOA is the next step in the maturing process of information technology, or rather: a next step in information technology and the way it should be used by organizations. All prior initiatives have somehow aligned, and have been incorporated in the fuzzy (and bloated?) perception of SOA. Best practices and proven concepts in architecture, software development, governance, alignment, and technology all converge when talking about Service Oriented Architecture.

3.3 The time is right

How did SOA become such a hype? Why did it gain interest so quickly? There are several reasons for this, and it's the combination of developments that triggered the massive interest (and the subsequent emergence of new insights into the workings of the internet and organizations in general). First there were technological initiatives along the lines of the integration of systems and 'web services'; second, there was a critical mass of internet usage; and maybe most importantly, there was very high pressure from business on IT to lower the total cost of ownership (TCO) and to increase performance and reliability. After SOA started receiving interest, the rapid adoption by software vendors increased the presence of the SOA acronym in marketing and sales, thus building up a hype. Expanding from technology, the real business value of SOA became clear, as well as the potentially positive impact on businesses.

However, it does not only involve marketing and sales. The reason SOA has been accepted and introduced into more and more organizations is that it is a clear model that addresses real IT problems. It is 'the right way' of doing IT and also 'feels' right to people that have to deal with IT. It feels right because the concepts that make up SOA are easy and well known.

3.4 The seven easy concepts of SOA

Based on real-life IT experience from the past 40 years or so, we can now say there are certain ways to do IT properly. If you were to do all these things, you would end up 'inventing' SOA. In fact many companies have already been practising the SOA principles for years, even prior to the time when the term 'SOA' was first introduced.

The easy concepts are:

1. Componentize
   To prevent things from becoming messy, you naturally group things and define components.
2. Agree on how to do things
   When doing business, you probably try to agree with staff on the way you work together, agree with suppliers on delivery, etc.
3. Use what you already have
   Before you buy something new, you first see if something you already have fits the need.
4. From 'made to order' to 'infrastructure'
   If there's a fitting ready-made solution on the shelf, it is better to use that than have one built specifically for you.
5. Facilitate change, continually improve
   The only thing that won't change, is change itself. So you probably rely on the fact that eventually some things will change.
6. Do it for a (business) reason
   When spending money, you want to know what you are getting in return.
7. React to the environment
   While a bit similar to 'facilitate change', reacting to the environment is the day-to-day business: if something happens, you want to respond in such a way that is best for the company.

We will now demonstrate how these concepts make up SOA. In the course of the explanation we shall also delve into concepts like the enterprise service bus, layering, event-driven architecture, and some acronyms commonly used when discussing SOA.

3.4.1 Easy concept 1: Componentize

The most commonly agreed aspect of SOA is the fact that Service Oriented Architecture is made up of services. From an IT viewpoint, services are small blocks of processing that can be called upon to do some work. From a business viewpoint, a service is 'something that we do in order to add value', probably supported by IT. With SOA, the two viewpoints coincide: a service being a small block of processing that can be called upon to support something the business does in order to add value.

If we look at IT in general as it supports the business processes, there are clear reasons for wanting to split things up. We do not want to have one large blob of technology that is hard to understand and difficult to maintain. We do not want everything to be so closely knit together that we can't change one bit without impacting many or all of the others. And finally, there's a very pragmatic argument for splitting things up: you just can't manage creating one big system to support your entire organization.

To address this need to split things up in the best way possible, SOA-based IT will, by definition, have two properties:
- Services are as independent of each other as possible.
- Services are defined along lines that make sense businesswise.

Services are as independent of each other as possible
Here, 'independent' refers to: independent in design, but also independent while in operation. Independence in design offers us the ability to change one service without necessarily changing all others. This independence is reached by designing services in such a way that each service can operate without relying on others, or, when reliance is key, by defining a flexible connection between the two services that will not break when small changes happen. Here XML, a flexible and extendable format for sending data, fits in perfectly.

Operational independence is also achieved by trying to be asynchronous as much as possible: services are no longer waiting for one another to finish processing, but rather they are just 'waiting to be told' that something has to be done. A service does a bit of processing, and then forwards the results to a following service that also does some processing. Once a bit of processing is done, the service 'forgets' all about it and is ready to handle another request or call. It's a bit like how air traffic controllers work: if an airplane is 'in their control' they know all about it, keep it safe, and guide it through airspace. Once an airplane crosses some boundary, or gets closer to an airport, the plane is handed over to another controller. The first controller then 'forgets' all about the plane and is ready to handle another one. Making SOA as asynchronous as possible constitutes a great difference to traditional, so called 'online', ways of performing processing. 'Loosely coupled' is a frequently used term to describe this independence of services.

A great challenge in designing Service Oriented Architecture is to define services that are loosely coupled yet still have enough cohesion to make it possible to form complex processes easily.

Services are defined along lines that make sense businesswise

Once you start thinking about services, an important question intimately related to SOA pops up: how do I determine how large the services, the parts of the system, should be? How should they be defined?

There is a lot that can be said on *how*, but there's one most important best practice that is used to define services: a service should make sense *business-wise*. In a way, IT is a technological abstraction of the business it supports. A business process is supported by technical processes, a business action results in IT actions taking place. The closer this abstraction resembles reality, the better it fits the movements and operation of the business. With SOA, we're looking to divide up all the IT in such a way that it mirrors the business as closely as possible.

This may sound simple, but doesn't work all the way down. At the lowest level, IT still consists of bits of code being executed on some machine. At that level, it may be hard to recognize the business process that is being executed. We'll have to admit that there may also be services that are too technical to make business sense. This leads to the discovery that there are multiple layers in SOA, much like there were layers in previous architectural models of client-server or internet applications. IT is made up of different levels, the highest being the 'business level', the lowest relating to hardware and low-level code.

To summarize: Service Oriented Architecture is an architecture in which we strive to create services that make business sense and are loosely coupled.

3.4.2 Easy concept 2: Agree on how to do things

Collaborating with partners, different departments and different customers takes a lot of work. All groups require different things, have different expectations of what they may achieve, and are willing to do different things for you or your company. Integration is difficult.

In a typical IT environment there are many different systems that are used to support day-to-day business. When integrating or communicating on a business level, the underlying systems will also have to be integrated or start communicating. Again, we see that IT mirrors the business side of an organization. The work that has to be done on a business level will also be done at IT level.

Enterprise Application Integration (EAI) is a concept slightly older than SOA. While EAI, much like SOA, is also a fuzzy term that has been hyped, it was invented for the same reasons that one now proposes SOA. The main goal of EAI is integrating all IT into one, in order to be more flexible and more efficient.

Service Oriented Architecture uses many of the best practices developed in the field of EAI. The most notable of these are two important realizations that are incorporated in any successful SOA:
- Standards.
- Integration of data.

Standards are important

Agreements are common understandings between two or more parties. When using software, the more parties adhere to a certain agreement, the better it is: there is less chance you'll be trapped forever in the way one particular vendor solves a certain problem. An agreement becomes a 'standard' once enough parties agree to use the same solution or approach, or once an authoritative party declares it 'the standard'. On a technical level, this can be an agreement on how the messages that go across a network should be written; on a higher level it can be an agreement on how you can find services that are available within your network. Other methodological standards such as Rational Unified Process or project management methods turn out to be important when choosing the supporting tools or when aiming to recruit people with the right knowledge.

It is also possible to implement standards within one company or within a group of partners working together. For example, large retailers have specified the way suppliers must(!) supply information about their products: prescribing the messages and the way the messages should be delivered.

Integration of data is important

First, what do we mean by the 'integration' of data? Essentially it is a very old concept of agreeing on 'what means what'. If, in a certain corner of an organization, an order is assigned a number for identification, do all systems and departments recognize the same number? If one department reports a profit, can it directly be compared to the profit of another department, or does the one include different costs? To be able to translate data from one into another, it must be known how they relate. Note that this is a business question to be answered, implemented in technology that does the actual integration and/or translation.

Within the boundaries of one organization this can already be quite a challenge, especially if it is a large multinational company. To obtain unity in the understanding of data across organizations, industry standards are emerging, trying to agree on common terminology to be used when sending information between services within different organizations.

Again, there is nothing new about industry standards being developed (remember EDIFACT or SWIFT), but with SOA the benefits of standards are much greater.

The integration of financial data is helped along greatly by improved laws on reporting. For example, in a sense Sarbanes-Oxley introduces a reporting standard prescribed by law.

3.4.3 Easy concept 3: Use what you already have

Before making something new, you want to see if something you already have will address your need. Or, in a slightly different perspective, you don't want two departments doing more or less the same thing, if it could be done by one. This concept also applies to IT: we continually strive to do things only once. With SOA we're taking a step to find more and more pieces of IT that are normally implemented several times, so that we can now implement them only once.

The benefits of this decrease of redundancy are attractive:
• Less technology to maintain, so less cost. This benefit is especially attractive if you realize that a very large part of all IT budgets is currently spent on maintaining existing IT instead of on creating innovations.

- Less technology also means that changes are easier to make, thus adding to the speed with which IT can respond to the changing demand from the business, increasing the so-called *agility* of IT.
- Less everything: hardware cost, license fees, bugs and errors, skills to maintain, etc.

Earlier initiatives, like Object Orientation or Component Based Development have paved the way in thinking about reuse: experience tells us that the reusable components cannot be too small, and that it must be *easy* (for everyone, from business to IT) to reuse a component.

Reuse of services

If services are well designed, and loosely coupled, they can easily be reused. For reuse to be possible, a service must give predictable results (do what it is supposed to do) in whichever way it is called upon (this is called 'context independence'). For example, a service to support the registration of an accident for an insurance company is only really reusable if the same service can be used when registering by phone, by email, via an intermediary, or directly via the internet. If the service responds differently to each situation, there is little or no reuse.

The key to achieving reuse

SOA enables the reuse of services. For reuse to actually take place in your organization, SOA alone will not suffice. A suitable management approach and the right 'economy' for projects and reusable services must be created before reuse will really take off.

More than one way of reuse

In most discussions, reuse focuses on the most elementary type of reuse: using one service in multiple business processes. While it is an attractive manner of reuse, there are other ways that are more likely to happen, and probably more profitable. To explain this different view on reuse, we introduce the easy concept 'from made-to-order to infrastructure'.

3.4.4 Easy concept 4: From 'made to order' to 'infrastructure'

In the earliest days of IT, programmers had a lot to do. Even the simplest task had to be manually coded. Reading a file from a disk? Program it yourself!

Showing some text on a display? Program it yourself! Storing data somewhere to retrieve it later? Program it yourself!

Nowadays, you wouldn't imagine writing software that performs database-like actions. The same goes for many other basic bits that make up the toolkit of software developers: from web portals to user administration, from emailing facilities to spelling check routines. All these are simply available to use when creating software.

The effect of a whole industry adopting a common architecture, such as SOA, is that tooling and support can be made to address certain parts of the architecture. New tooling is becoming available to take care of the transport of messages, for security, and for all sorts of other general functionality. New layers of infrastructure are becoming available, just like database software previously became 'infrastructure'.

In a way, this is a best practice that is better known as 'buy before build'. With SOA it should become 'buy before reuse before build'. Note the order in which 'buy' and 'reuse' are put. This means: if some tooling is available on the market that will fill a need, it's better to use this tool than to even reuse an existing service. There's a reason for this: there's very little to no maintenance cost for a bought service: most to all maintenance is done by the supplier. With a real SOA, there's even the option to buy the service as a service: not buy software to install on your own machines and have your own people support it, but let the service reside elsewhere, and just agree on the service level that should be provided. Cutting down the maintenance cost of IT will immediately improve the total cost of ownership.

In this way, an organization will eventually grow an 'infrastructure' of services that can be used by anyone within the company to do new or existing things. It will be a large set of services that are 'just available' to pick from when doing projects. Note that a 'project' will become smaller, because less effort has to be put into creating the services. Smaller projects mean faster time to market, which will have an impact on the way business will use IT. It might become possible to 'just try' things, to see if they provide benefits: if it's fast and cheap to try a new process, why not try to see if it works as promised!

A long-term ambition of IT: agile development, developing interactively with the business, comes within reach.

Reuse and infrastructural services

To show the different ways of thinking about reuse, we have taken the example of a hospital, where services can be used to support day-to-day operations in taking care of patients.

In a real life situation, in which different departments have chosen their own systems, as shown in Figure 3.1, these systems will work together with difficulty. Although these systems mirror the organizational structure and there are some gaps, there is also some overlap: redundancy of data, manual keying of data, double entries, etc.

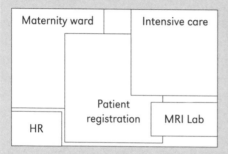

Figure 3.1 Traditional situation

Then, with SOA, as in Figure 3.2, there's a more solid and coherent IT supporting the business. Services are directly linked to business capabilities, and can be reused in different projects, processes, and across the organization. All information will be entered once, all information can be accessed where needed.

Reuse

IT Diet and feeding	Operating	Medication	Diagnosis	Patient registration	⋮	⋮	⋮	⋮

Figure 3.2 Business services

The other way in which SOA accomplishes reuse is by separating out the common services needed in many different business services. These common services, shown in Figure 3.3, can then be implemented using standard tooling, thus increasing development speed and decreasing maintenance cost.

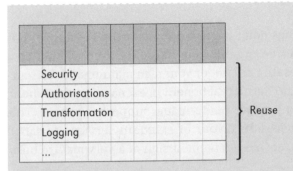

Figure 3.3 Technical services

Business services are composed of technical services, sometimes enhanced with some specific programming or configuration. This doesn't matter to business, as long as the business service can be used to support business functions directly. Underneath the bonnet there can be technical services, legacy applications, existing CRM systems, etc. The complete picture resembles Figure 3.4.

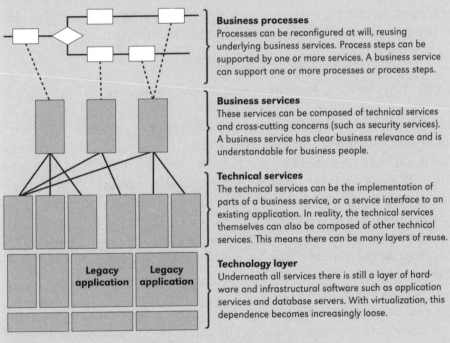

Business processes
Processes can be reconfigured at will, reusing underlying business services. Process steps can be supported by one or more services. A business service can support one or more processes or process steps.

Business services
These services can be composed of technical services and cross-cutting concerns (such as security services). A business service has clear business relevance and is understandable for business people.

Technical services
The technical services can be the implementation of parts of a business service, or a service interface to an existing application. In reality, the technical services themselves can also be composed of other technical services. This means there can be many layers of reuse.

Technology layer
Underneath all services there is still a layer of hardware and infrastructural software such as application services and database servers. With virtualization, this dependence becomes increasingly loose.

Figure 3.4 Services and layers in Service Oriented Architecture

Proactive destruction

As with reuse in general: things don't happen automatically. For a real opti-mization of the set of services an organization harbours, there should be a regular check to see if services that are under your own maintenance are cur-rently available on the market. There's real benefit in exchanging a self-built, self-maintained service for a bought, ready-made, supported service. This destruction of your own services, in favour of standard services, is called 'proactive destruction' and is, despite its name, a sign of a very mature busi-ness IT organization.

The challenge

When analysing an organization and deciding which services are necessary, much attention will be devoted to the 'added value' an organization provides: if I can build my entire organization out of services provided by third parties, how do I differ from my competitors? If any competitor can put together the same services as I'm using, what's the difference to our end customer? The difference can be in several things: the same services can be used with dif-ferent parameters (different business rules), in a different process or – and we see this a lot – with different labelling and marketing.

3.4.5 Easy concept 5: Facilitate change, continually improve

'The only thing that will not change is change itself.' Predicting the future is pretty hard to do. Yet for IT to be of value, it must harmonize with the business that it supports. So to have a good fit, both now and in the hard-to-predict future, IT must be able to change: it must be able to adapt to changing cir-cumstances, it must 'facilitate business change'. Facilitating change simply means: responding to new circumstances quickly and in the best way possible. There are two ingredients here: one is the ability to change (the agility) and the other is the capability to keep finding the optimum, to continually improve.

The easy concepts of 'componentize' and 'from made-to-order to infrastruc-ture' contribute largely to realizing the agility that is needed. An essential feature of this agility is that some things don't change. In order to put together some building blocks quickly, the building blocks themselves should be fairly stable.

The continuous improvement is embodied in initiatives like CMM or Six Sigma. Even ITIL, the common library of practices for infrastructure support, includes an optimization process. With SOA, the development of software, the use of design methods, and the greater use of reusable services all neatly fit into a process improvement approach. With SOA, combined with factory-like software development methods, IT can start to automate its own processes, thus increasing productivity, decreasing the risk of errors, and embedding knowledge in processes and tooling.

3.4.6 Easy concept 6: Do it for a (business) reason

The relationship between IT and business has always been difficult. When a project takes too long to complete, it's hard to stay in line with the developing business demand. Scope creep is common, because business does not stop thinking once a project has started. One thing we have learned over the years is that the 'success' of IT is measured only in how much the business demand is met. Managing expectations has become important to IT, but even more important is delivering the solutions the business needs.

With SOA we have addressed these issues: increasing agility to deliver faster and to develop software that, by definition, is in line with business.

Traditionally, the applications developed are defined by organizational boundaries: by department, by product, or by what was available from the market. This means people in real processes are regularly using several systems to fulfil one request, or to finish one process. Look up something in one system, change something in another, and report about it in a third. This is far from ideal. This is also the reason that Enterprise Application Integration has been a desired goal for years.

With SOA we finally get it right: by defining services that support real business functions ('capabilities'). These business functions will be fairly stable over time, have a direct link to what the business does, and are a lot less dependent on the way a company is internally organized. Ownership is logically attributed to the business unit or people supplying the business function. Because of the direct business relation, services can be grouped together to provide more complex business functions, just as multiple units can work together to provide more difficult services to customers or partners.

In a way, the 'services' model of units providing a service behind a well-defined interface could also apply to the people part of organizations (thus achieving the 'Service Oriented Enterprise'). Using email to send out requests to different units and divisions, a similar pattern will arise as when IT systems are performing IT services.

With the rise of SOA, the awareness of IT people of the importance of business drivers, the business goals behind IT, is greater than ever. Most 'technical' aspects are provided by the new layers of infrastructure, and all attention is devoted to business processes, business rules, and definition of business services.

Changing role of IT

IT is more business-oriented than before, and this brings us to 'alignment': aligning business and IT along the same goals. Alignment in real life isn't easy. It's already difficult for business units to align and communicate regularly among one another. It's no different between business and IT: a lot of effort must be put into keeping the two aligned. Only when there's a 'strategic dialogue' on the long and short-term goals can any improvement be expected in the way business and IT work together.

IT needs a clear view of the business plans in order to consider which services to provide, but also to decide on the quality to be delivered. SOA gives us the opportunity to invest in services that are more valuable and more important, and to save money on services that are less critical. To make these decisions, IT must know what the business expects, and what to expect in the (near) future. Different strategies will result in different choices at IT level: for example, internationalization will result in new languages and currencies, takeovers will result in data integration and infrastructure consolidation, new products will result in new services, new processes, and more extensive management reporting.

Again: most concepts aren't new. Business focus has been a practice of successful IT departments for years, and IT has been trying to make IT mirror business whenever possible. With SOA, the architecture makes it a lot easier: the tooling support will (almost naturally) encourage even programmers to refocus on the business issues, while the services are a neat way of dividing up IT along the lines of business functions.

3.4.7 Easy concept 7: React to the environment

IT must adapt to changing circumstances; it must display the much needed agility. On a more day-to-day level, there is a more basic requirement for IT: it must respond to things that happen. When a customer calls the service desk to place a new order, something should be happening inside the organization. If someone in the warehouse accidentally drops a container of vases, some process should start up to replace these before a customer comes to collect them. Present day businesses are put under pressure by customers and partners to respond quickly to business events. Delivery times are generally measured in days or hours instead of weeks or months. The use of the internet, with its implicit promise of 'immediate response' to requests, only adds to this pressure. It's a bit like the change from paper mail to email: new technology creates new expectations.

This has an impact on the way people work in an organization, and on IT. Saving up orders, and synchronizing these in a weekly batch is no longer possible. Insight into stocks has to be accurate to at least a day, but preferably to the hour or to the minute. Synchronization across a value chain containing several parties can no longer be done by telephone or email. The practice has become to implement processes in real-time, straight through fashion. Any event, like an online order, change or request, is taken up as soon as it occurs.

The benefits are that management can use more accurate information for taking business decisions and customers get the service they expect.

An essential element in this higher response rate is the integration of all IT systems involved in handling the events. Usually this also means a change of architecture: from batch to 'event-driven architecture'. It means loosely coupled services that can communicate with each other in an agreed way, and which can be configured to handle events at the moment they occur.

3.5 Summary

These easy concepts combine to make a powerful architecture that can address lots of problems existing in present day IT environments. It combines all best practices invented to solve the common problems that arise when designing technology to match the workings of any dynamic, organic business.

When an organization is using well-componentized services, which have been designed to support real business processes, which can communicate through well-agreed standards, and are designed to be reusable, maintainable and ready for the future, it can respond quickly to day-to-day events, and adapt smoothly to new markets and circumstances. IT will then be optimized to deliver the best TCO, and can regain its role of supporting and inspiring business in the quest for new and better business opportunities.

Making an organization adhere to standards and follow best practices is never easy. SOA is no different, but with SOA it's a matter of survival: without proper governance and a loose way of implementing standards, SOA will most certainly result in a larger mess than where you started from. So there's a lot to be gained. In the next chapter we'll discuss how to govern the concepts of SOA to success.

4 Govern or end up in a mess

4.1 Introduction

Now that you know what SOA means and that you can make money with it, let us start explaining how to implement it. What is the most important requirement for the successful implementation of SOA? What is the number one thing that you need to take care of in order to make money with SOA? The answer is: governance.

Governance is by far the most important requirement. The absence of clear governance will inevitably lead to a quagmire of services. A lack of SOA Governance forms the greatest risk to the success of SOA projects. Governance is important enough to zoom in closely on the details of what it is and how you can implement it. This chapter introduces Enterprise Governance and Enterprise Architecture as the two most important success factors when implementing SOA.

4.2 Why is SOA Governance important?

The first question we have to answer is: why is governance so important in relation to SOA? Why is there such a great need for governance?

An important driver for SOA Governance is the reuse of services. One of the objectives of SOA implementation is to reduce costs by reusing services. Experience in the OO and CBD world has taught us that it is not easy to reuse objects and components. Reuse doesn't happen of its own accord. It has to be planned and meticulously managed. Despite all the best intentions, projects have been largely responsible for determining, quite autonomously, how functionality is delivered. It is often much easier for a project to develop components from scratch rather than trying to find the owners of reusable components (that is, if the owners are actually known) and then request those components for reuse and make the necessary arrangements. We now have to take the lessons learned in the OO and CBD area and make sure that the reuse of services becomes a success. This requires policies and management.

A proper design of services is another important factor for SOA Governance. The same applies to designing business processes. In real-life practice, the design of business processes and services will often go hand in hand. Policies are necessary in order to ensure that services and processes are designed in a standard manner.

Another important driver is the need to manage complexity. Unmanaged IT investments in the past have led to a great diversity in applications, software and hardware. The consequence is that the IT environment has become increasingly complex, making changes very costly and time consuming.

The duality of SOA implementation is that, on the one hand, it helps resolve legacy complexity and increases flexibility and manoeuvrability, but, on the other, it is inherently complex because the larger blocks of functionality (applications) have to make way for many more smaller blocks of functionality (services). If managing hundreds of applications already seems a daunting task then the addition of hundreds of services is definitely going to seem overwhelming.

It is not yet clear how many services will be required for an organization that now has more than a thousand applications: hundreds or thousands? It all depends on the extent to which the services are implemented. One thing is certain: if we build and manage services in the same manner as we have managed applications in the past, the complexity will increase exponentially. Policies and management are vitally important in order to prevent this from happening.

The fourth and last driver that we shall mention here is the issue of investment and finance. SOA requires investment in infrastructure and expertise. The problem is that many initial costs are going to hit the first SOA project that is realized, which has a large and negative influence on the business case for that project. Additionally the first SOA projects will have a steeper learning curve, which will increase costs and project duration in comparison to subsequent projects that will profit from their efforts. This makes it important to view investments in SOA and infrastructure projects not in isolation but rather in their relationship to one another. Accordingly, it is necessary to manage the investments as a portfolio. Policies, principles and management are definitely needed for this, as well as for judging whether or not the portfolio is right.

In a more general context, it can be stated that SOA Governance is an absolute precondition for the realization of the promised business value of SOA. Business flexibility and cost reduction do not occur of their own accord, but are the result of purposeful steering.

The need for SOA Governance is no different from the need for IT Governance. The drivers we mentioned – cost reduction, flexibility increase, and viewing investments as a portfolio – are nothing new. They were also the drivers at the inception of IT Governance. What is important now is to ensure the proactive adoption of SOA Governance before it becomes a problem, as was done with IT Governance.

The following two figures display the difference between SOA with governance and SOA without [Weblayers 2005b].

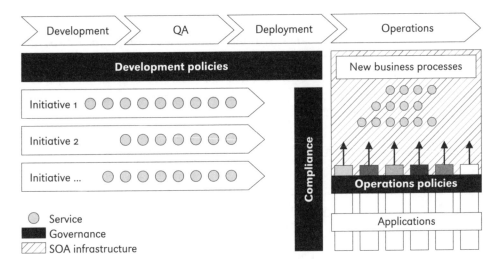

Figure 4.1 SOA with governance

Figure 4.1 shows that there is a set of services (the light grey dots) that are independent of the applications that supply these services to the business processes. The governance that has been set up to achieve this consists of development and operations policies and the supervision and control of their compliance. The policies are also referred to as 'architectural principles' and are a part of the enterprise architecture of the organization.

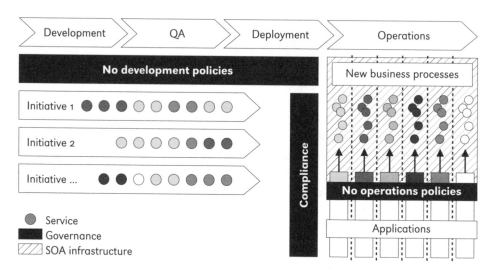

Figure 4.2 SOA without governance

In a situation without governance, without policies and compliance thus, the organization may suffer from the creation of services that are application-oriented and thus offer little or no chance of reuse. In addition, services are built in all different kinds of ways, ultimately resulting in a complex, expensive, and very ineffective IT.

Figure 4.3 shows the need for governance and architecture from a historical perspective.

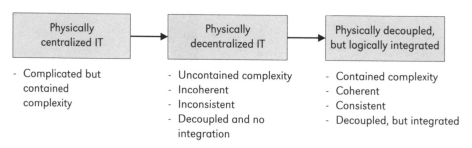

Figure 4.3 Changing complexity in IT

In the seventies and eighties of the previous century, IT was physically centralized. This ensured that complexity could be held in check. From the nineties onward, IT became increasingly decentralized, partly under the influence of the possibilities offered by Client/Server technology. This eventually led to an enormous growth in complexity that could not be stemmed. The result is that nowadays many organizations have a physically decentralized IT. This is the root of many integration headaches because processes and systems are not consistent and coherent, and have become increasingly complex in the course of time. In order to arrive at a logically integrated business and IT landscape, it is of the utmost importance to have governance and architectural competency at one's disposal. This is the only way one can work toward a situation in which physically separated components can work together logically, in an optimum manner, and in which the complexity is manageable.

In conclusion, we quote Gartner [Gartner 2006d], who typifies the three situations that can arise without SOA Governance:

- Wild West SOA.
  This happens when services are introduced in a big way without any form of coordination. Nobody knows how many services have been implemented; where they can be found and how they can be reused. In this case there is a huge need for a management function that can handle the coordination. Rules are necessary to manage the coordination of building and maintaining the services.
- Duplicated SOA.
  This situation is a little more disciplined than a 'Wild West SOA'. However there are too many services that partially or completely overlap each other's functionality. Evidently it is not possible to mandate reuse. In this situation there may be rules for building and maintaining services but there is no system in place to enforce reusability. The result is a situation in which many services are duplicated.
- Purchased SOA.
  There is a SOA infrastructure in place, but it is hardly used. This is a situation where there is little buy-in from the business units and no commitment to use services. What is needed here is more involvement within the organization and clarity on who is responsible for the SOA success in this organization.

The picture is clear. With a lack of effective SOA Governance, all the potential advantages of SOA will remain out of reach. Furthermore, it is not inconceivable that an IT situation will arise that is worse than the initial situation, despite all the investment: less flexibility, less reuse, and a completely impenetrable mass of thousands of services in which no one knows how it all works.

4.3 What is SOA Governance?

What is SOA Governance exactly, and how is it related to other forms of governance? Let us start with the 'highest form' of governance in an organization, namely, Enterprise Governance. 'Enterprise Governance is the organizational competence for exercising continuous guiding authority regarding enterprise strategy development, and subsequent design, implementation and operation of the enterprise.' [Hoogervorst 2007]

The most important aim of Enterprise Governance is to ensure that the organization's strategy is actually realized. Many strategic initiatives fail. Kaplan and Norton articulate this as follows: 'Various studies indicate that 70 per cent to 90 per cent of organizations failed to realize success from their strategies.' This failure is largely caused by a lack of consistency and coherence in the implementation of the strategy. The function of Enterprise Governance is precisely to ensure that strategic initiatives are converted into action in a consistent and coherent manner. Enterprise architecture is the competency that is required to guarantee consistency and coherence.

Figure 4.4 shows the relation between Enterprise, IT, and SOA Governance. Enterprise Governance refers to the steering of the products and services that the organization supplies to the outside world. IT Governance is an integral component of Enterprise Governance but is limited to the steering of IT products and services. 'IT Governance is the organizational competence for exercising continuous guiding authority regarding IT strategy development, and subsequent design, implementation and operation of IT systems.' [Hoogervorst 2007]

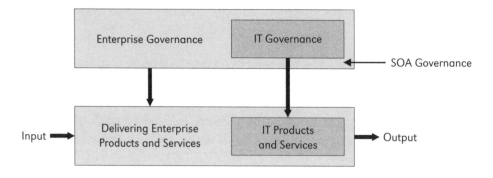

Figure 4.4 Relationship between Enterprise, IT, and SOA Governance

SOA Governance is related not only to the IT domain, but also extends up to enterprise level. Figure 4.5 displays the governance subareas that are influenced by the introduction of SOA.

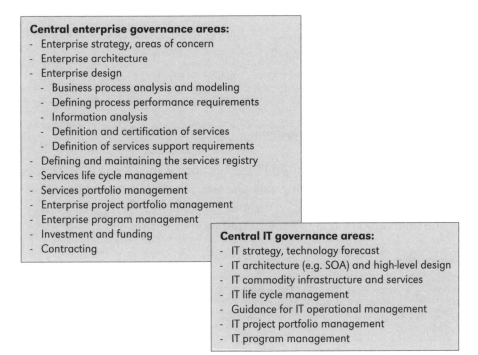

Central enterprise governance areas:
- Enterprise strategy, areas of concern
- Enterprise architecture
- Enterprise design
  - Business process analysis and modeling
  - Defining process performance requirements
  - Information analysis
  - Definition and certification of services
  - Definition of services support requirements
- Defining and maintaining the services registry
- Services life cycle management
- Services portfolio management
- Enterprise project portfolio management
- Enterprise program management
- Investment and funding
- Contracting

Central IT governance areas:
- IT strategy, technology forecast
- IT architecture (e.g. SOA) and high-level design
- IT commodity infrastructure and services
- IT life cycle management
- Guidance for IT operational management
- IT project portfolio management
- IT program management

Figure 4.5 Governance areas influenced by SOA

The areas of concern mentioned in Figure 4.5 are not only important in the implementation of SOA but are also essential for the implementation of the business objectives of an organization in a mutually coherent manner. The implementation of SOA is much more straightforward in an organization whose governance functions properly and which has embedded mechanisms for portfolio management, for example, or decisions on investment.

We do not regard SOA Governance as a separate form of governance. The implementation of SOA requires an organization to have its Enterprise and IT Governance functioning properly, allowing scope for the introduction of services that entail a number of new governance areas, such as Services Life Cycle Management and Services Portfolio Management.

Finally, we wish to point out the difference between governance and management. Governance refers to the organization of the steering process, while management is concerned with the execution of the steering processes that make use of governance mechanisms and structures.

The following sections deal in more depth with a number of specific SOA Governance areas:

- Services Portfolio Management.
- Services Life Cycle Management.
- Services Registry.

4.4 Services Portfolio Management

One of the primary subjects within IT Governance is the IT portfolio. This, in its simplest form, is a list showing data on costs, benefits, risks, and the coherence between the desired changes, ongoing projects, and the regular management and maintenance of applications and infrastructure.

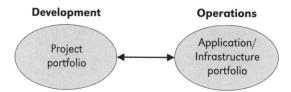

Figure 4.6 Governance portfolios

The IT portfolio consists of two parts. One part is devoted to change: the project portfolio, whereas the other part is devoted to maintaining the status quo: the application and infrastructure portfolio. Both portfolios have to be managed. That means that a project must not only be assessed on its merits, but also in the way it relates to the total set of projects. After all, it's possible that two projects, viewed independently, might provide a definite added value, but would actually conflict when viewed from a portfolio perspective. The same can be said for the total set of applications and infrastructures. Those require management as well, not only by looking at individual licences but also by looking at the portfolio. That will reveal any overlaps. So when looking at an application portfolio, you would ideally want to see only one application per block of functionality.

SOA adds an important management item to Figure 4.6, namely the service portfolio, as can be seen in Figure 4.7.

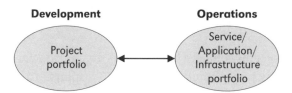

Figure 4.7 Governance portfolios supplemented by the service portfolio

An application is a specific set of computer software that allots certain capabilities of a computer directly to several tasks that the user wishes to perform. A service is an autonomous and recognizable (for the business) task delivered by an application or application component. SOA actually introduces another layer, that of services.

Just as with applications and infrastructures, it is important to manage the services as a portfolio. That means that decisions have to be made relating to:
- Which services are required?
- Which services are required first?
- Does the service meet the defined criteria?
- Who pays for the creation and maintenance of the service?
- Who is the owner of the service?

In practice, it's all about managing the services portfolio. SOA Governance has to prevent uncontrolled growth in the portfolio. Additionally, SOA Governance has to ensure that the portfolio always contains a consistent and coherent set of services that reflect the requirements of the organization, taking into account the entire services life cycle.

The advantage of managing services as a portfolio is that, eventually, the application and infrastructure portfolios are less significant in the discussion between business and IT. If the functionality of an organization is built up out of services, then costs, benefits, risks, and coherence can be assigned to services, even if these services are delivered by legacy applications. The services need to deliver the functionality defined by the business under certain conditions. This is documented in service descriptions that form the basis for agreements on budgets, investments, and maintenance contracts.

The question who should manage the services portfolio is an interesting one. We believe that this is a business responsibility. After all, a service is a piece of business functionality that is used in a business process. It is quite possible that the business delegate this responsibility to IT.

Applications and infrastructure don't disappear when services are introduced. Managing them remains a necessity, but becomes purely an IT responsibility and is therefore not a point of negotiation between business and IT. The advantage of this is that the dialogue between business and IT becomes simpler and clearer. The disadvantage is that IT Governance doesn't get any easier with the introduction of SOA. This represents another reason to address SOA Governance.

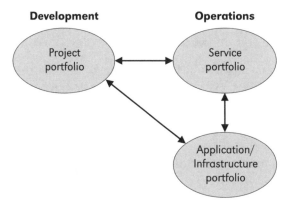

Figure 4.8 Service portfolio as primary portfolio

4.5 Services Life Cycle Management

Services Life Cycle Management is an important area of concern in governance. In fact, an organization should manage the life cycle of all its assets. This is a commonly accepted practice for capital goods such as buildings and machines. In the domain of IT, however, life cycle management is still in its infancy. It is a major problem in the field of applications in particular. In the course of time many applications have been realized within many organizations and only a few have been laid to rest. To a certain extent, this problem has been caused by the fact that new applications have taken over the functionality of other applications, but this is not always the case. As long as a limited part of the functionalities are needed, the application cannot be phased out. This will be easier with services because they represent only a limited piece of functionality. As a result, it will be easier to assess whether or not a service should be phased out. On the other hand, the services also create a problem inasmuch as the service can be used by various users. Here, too, as long as a service is being used by one customer, it cannot be phased out.

Figure 4.9 displays the life cycle of a service.

Figure 4.9 Life cycle of a service

Table 4.1 describes the various stages of a service.

State	Description
Planned	The service is included in the planning. It indicates that there is an intention to introduce the service. The service is described in general terms and assigned to a domain (system domain or business domain).
Specified	The service has a complete formal specification (logic, quality of service, and condition). See the following section in this chapter.
Being developed	The service is under development.
Provisioned	The service is ready for certification. The developers have completed the construction, tests, and documentation.
Operationally accepted	The service has been approved by the department that is responsible for the operation.

State	Description
Certified	The service fulfils the quality criteria. This applies to aspects such as function, performance, documentation (service description) and acceptability for operation. This is determined independently of the developers.
Published	The service is available for consumption. The service is now subjected to change control, operations, and monitoring.
Operational	The service is actually used in the production environment. The execution and the use are monitored, and production problems are tackled.
Obsolete	The service is no longer offered to new consumers. The current consumers are advised to switch over to alternatives as soon as possible. The non-committal nature of this depends on the situation.
Retired	The service is no longer used and can be removed from the register.

Table 4.1 States in the Service Life Cycle

As soon as a service has been identified, it should be included in the service portfolio. Only when the service has actually been removed can it also be taken out of the portfolio.

Services Life Cycle Management is a responsibility of the business. The same argumentation that is valid for Service Portfolio Management also applies here, namely, that a service is a piece of business functionality that is used in a business process. If, for example, an order-processing process uses a service that displays customer data, the ownership of the 'display customer data' service is a business responsibility that could be assigned to a marketing and sales section.

4.6 Services Registry

The Services Registry is the center where all services are registered. A Service Description of every service should be kept. Figure 4.10 shows the substance of this kind of description.

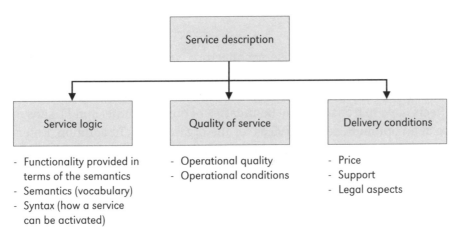

Figure 4.10 Service description

First of all, there is a description of what the service does, the service logic. This logic describes the functionality that the provider of the service must offer, along with a description of how the consumer can activate the service.

Then the quality of service is described. This defines the operational conditions under which the services are supplied by the provider. The nonfunctional requirements of the service, such as availability, reliability and scalability, determine the quality. The limitations of the service must also be apparent, such as the maximum number of simultaneous users, for example.

Finally, the conditions of delivery must also be agreed, such as the price of the service, the conditions that the provider must fulfil to guarantee payment, and agreements regarding support and liability.

Besides the Service Description it is essential to specify the owner of the service, the provider of the service, and the consumers of the service.

By maintaining a central registry, the conditions are created for possible reuse. Consulting the registry makes it clear to potential consumers which services are available, the conditions under which they can be used, and who should be approached if they actually wish to use the services. A registry is also essential for Service Life Cycle Management.

4.7 Enterprise Architecture

Figure 4.5 shows that Enterprise Architecture is an area of concern within Enterprise Governance, and an important one at that. Enterprise Architecture is an indispensable competency in the implementation of SOA. The enterprise architects have to transcend the boundaries of business units and IT silos to arrive at an optimum set of services for the organization. In addition, Enterprise Architecture offers the processes and products that are necessary to ensure the execution of the organization's strategy. Sogeti's Dynamic Enterprise Architecture [Berg 2006a] offers a working model that is very useful for working with Enterprise Architecture in an organization and in particular for the implementation of SOA. As we saw earlier, SOA is an architectural style and it is the enterprise architect who should engage in discussions about this in the organization.

4.7.1 A model for Enterprise Architecture

Dynamic Enterprise Architecture (DYA) contains a model that is highly applicable to SOA implementations. It is a 'skeleton' around which SOA implementations can be built and by means of which the significance of SOA for an organization can be determined: how to initiate one, and which resources will be required.

The core of the DYA Model consists of four processes covering the entire process of change, from strategy formation to realization:

- *Strategic Dialogue* – through which the business goals are established and elaborated into concrete project proposals by means of business cases. The business goals are discussed in a dialogue between business and IT.
- *Architectural Services* – the processes in which the architecture is formulated and then made available to the Strategic Dialogue and Development with Architecture processes.
- *Development with Architecture* – in which the business goals are achieved within the stipulated time frames and in accordance with the anticipated quality and costs – in the DYA process, Development with Architecture is the standard.
- *Development without Architecture* – a deliberate choice in special circumstances, perhaps involving extreme time pressure, to deviate from the architectural framework.

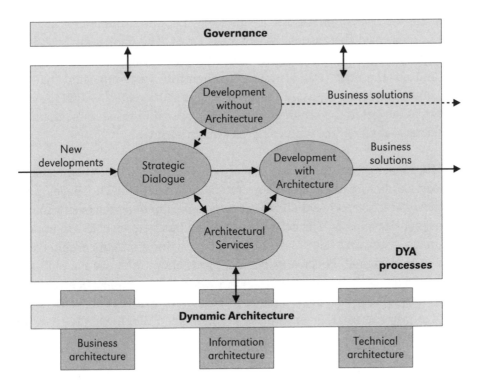

Figure 4.11 DYA model

In this model, Architectural Services (i.e., the development and maintenance of architecture) clearly constitute a support process. Architecture is not a goal in itself but a tool for managing the changes formulated in the Strategic Dialogue and realized in Development with(out) Architecture. It aligns these changes so they can best serve the business goals of the organization. Because the DYA Model clearly identifies the factors involved in architectural practices, it has been adopted by many organizations.

4.7.2 Using DYA for SOA

Using DYA terms, the decision whether or not to adopt SOA is made in the Strategic Dialogue. The Enterprise Architect supports the Strategic Dialogue by providing the principles and models that are needed to achieve the business goals while also ensuring a degree of mutual coherence. SOA principles and models are part of the standard baggage of the enterprise architect. He needs to outline the advantages and disadvantages of a SOA architectural style in relation to achieving the business goals of the organization. It is ultimately the top management that needs to decide about implementing the business goals and the associated business cases. The choice for SOA is a logical consequence of the business goals that an organization defines for itself, and not the other way around. It is therefore very important that an organization has at its disposal Enterprise Architecture expertise that has the wherewithal to get to the bottom of all the SOA capabilities and use them in discussions regarding the achievement of business goals.

The DYA model offers the possibility of benefiting from the advantages of using services before the necessary architecture is complete. The 'Developing without Architecture' process allows services to be implemented even without any design principles. In this case, of course, the business level has to understand that a clean-up cycle is required to fit everything into the architecture that is to be designed. Because policy decisions about SOA are made in the 'Strategic Dialogue', a consideration can be made between project needs (using services now) and organizational needs (invest later in order to allow the services to fit into the broader enterprise architecture). Whatever the case, an unbridled growth of services outside the architecture has to be prevented.

Using the DYA model relative to SOA has the following advantages:
- It clearly points out that SOA is not a goal but a means to achieve a business objective. SOA is an architectural style that can function as an enabler. The SOA must be discussed in the Strategic Dialogue.
- SOA is implemented using the 'just in time, just enough' principle, as this is driven by the organizational business objectives. DYA provides a model in which the business objectives drive the SOA implementation.
- DYA makes governance and architecture practical and actionable. It provides a method to address these two very important competencies, which are essential for succesfull SOA. With DYA, the concepts and visions relating to architecture and governance find their way into execution of projects and the day-to-day operation.
- There is the flexibility to embark on a SOA project without architecture, but there needs to be proper consideration of the fact that the developed services will need to be brought under architecture at a later stage.

Should an organization plan to implement SOA in a big way, such as a strategic transformation of the organization, it will first have to conduct a Strategic Dialogue which specifies the business objectives that are to be served by this transformation. Setting up a business vision regarding SOA is then a necessary part of the Strategic Dialogue.

Should an organization plan to implement SOA by starting small, with a single project, then it is still preferable to develop a business vision regarding SOA. If nothing else, one should at least decide at what point in time it will be required. The problem is that not every separate project is waiting for a SOA vision and will advance whatever the situation. You will need at least a minimum base of Governance and Architecture, otherwise the SOA implementation will inevitably lead to an increase in complexity with the associated maintenance costs.

In short, whether you are embarking on a big or small SOA journey, the first step required is a Strategic Dialogue.

In addition to defining a business vision during the Strategic Dialogue, business cases and plans for starting one or more SOA projects are also made. Parts of the architecture can be drafted using specific methodologies, along with best practices such as industry models. Entry points (People, Information, Process, Reuse, and Connectivity) can be used to identify triggers and business objectives for specific SOA projects. These are discussed in Chapter 9. Furthermore, topics like training and research into the tools required can be addressed at this stage. As the SOA Maturity Model (which will be introduced in Chapter 8) will demonstrate, the implementation of SOA will create an avalanche of consequences.

Once again, all choices are entirely dependent on what an organization hopes to achieve with SOA and the chosen path. Should an organization decide to start small by implementing a few web services, it doesn't make sense to implement a methodology for business modeling. There is a specific time for everything. To summarize, Strategic Dialogue leads to well-considered investment decisions.

4.7.3 Different perspectives of architecture

How do different perspectives on Enterprise Architecture relate to SOA? In Architectural Services, architectures are formulated to support Strategic Dialogue and Development with Architecture. There are three types of architecture: one that supports strategic decision making, one that makes it possible to set up business cases, and a last one that provides the necessary framework for projects [Berg 2006a]. We will discuss these three types of architecture in the next sections.

Architecture for strategic decision making

In most cases, the first type of architecture (intended to facilitate strategic decision making) has a coordinating function. This architecture is meant to recognize shared features, position individual developments, and govern mutual coherence. It is used to channel the overall set of changes, but also to ensure that any infrastructural requirements are met on time. This form of architecture exists at a very high conceptual level, has broad scope, and serves as support for senior management in its strategic decision making. It is often called *city plan* or, especially in large holdings and multinational companies, *corporate architecture*. Regarding SOA, the city plan should identify domains where SOA can add value. A list of SOA principles and guidelines at enterprise level should also be part of the city plan. Guidelines can be developed in projects, but it is advisable to identify them beforehand and make them part of the enterprise architecture.

Architecture to set up business cases

Architecture intended to provide support at a tactical level for concrete business cases has a more straightforward steering function. It is used to ensure that individual changes actually occur in the desired manner. It often has a narrower scope (e.g., a business unit, business domain, or business programme) and goes into more depth when describing details. It is designated by the expression *domain architecture* and may have a specific name, such as *loans architecture*. When the decision has been taken that a domain will be service-based, domain architecture should provide guidance for implementing SOA in that domain. This can be done by modeling future architecture in terms of the business services to be provided by this domain. These services can then be mapped onto the existing application landscape to obtain an idea of the transformation required for this domain. Besides these functional domains, we can identify technical domains like integration, service management, and business intelligence. These domains describe the policies and guidelines to implement certain technologies or, more generally, how to deal with the domain with respect to technology. In the case of an organization deciding to implement SOA, this could be a separate technical domain for which policies and guidelines will be developed in order to realize a common set of agreements on how to implement SOA. The IBM SOA Reference Architecture contains a division into eleven areas for which choices must be made [IBM 2005b].

The use of SOA Reference Architecture

Reference architecture is a powerful aid in SOA implementation. In general terms, reference architecture shows the essential features of SOA-based architecture, in this particular case. The reference architecture presented in Figure 4.12 is from IBM and displays a division into eleven areas. This has a number of important advantages. With this kind of division, organizations can deploy the proper resources to meet the specific wishes and requirements of the areas, so that it is not necessary for everyone to be an expert in all environments. As a result, efficient use can be made of the available resources, training costs can be lowered, the correct toolsets can be used in every area, and new functionality can be implemented in a more efficient manner.

The primary areas in reference architecture are: Interaction, Process, Information, Partner, Business Application and Access. These are the domains of application software.

The other parts of reference architecture: Business Innovation & Optimization, Development, IT Service Management and Infrastructure are auxiliary to the primary areas. They are used to model the business design, to build and assemble software, implement applications, and manage the operational IT and business environment.

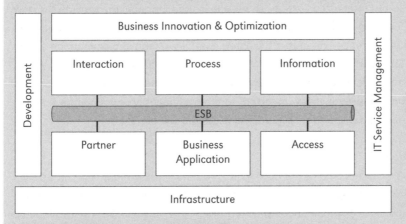

Figure 4.12 SOA Reference Architecture

If we examine the above mentioned areas of Interaction, Process and Information more specifically, we notice that these areas strongly resemble the traditional categorization into presentation logic, business logic and data logic. If Business Application is then regarded as a derivative of the Process area, n-tier distributed system architecture can be recognized.

We do not restrict the use of services in a particular SOA to the business logic alone. All the components of the application, including the presentation logic and data logic are regarded as services. A brief description of each area is given on the following pages.

Interaction

This area deals with the presentation logic of the business design components that support the interaction between the applications and the end users. Here, it must be observed that the interaction with the external world is not limited to human interaction alone. It is also possible to realize this by interaction logic with RFID and other industrial equipment such as sensors and vehicles. Authentication and authorization are an integral part of this area.

Process

This area includes various forms of compositional logic, the most notable of which are business process flows and business state machines (finite-state machines for business composition). We consider both kinds of composition mechanisms, plus other forms such as business rules and decision tree processing, as well as more *ad hoc* forms of composition, to be equally valid approaches to choreographing service composition.

Business Application

These provide the runtime services required for new application components to be included in the integrated system. These application components provide the new business logic required to adapt existing business processes to meet changing competitive and customer demands of the enterprise. Design and implementation of new business logic components for integration enables them to be fully reuseable, allowing them to participate in new and updated business processes over time. Business Application includes functions important to the traditional programmer for building maintainable, flexible, and reuseable business logic components.

Information

This area primarily contains the data logic of the business design. This can be seen from two different angles of approach. Seen from above, Information offers access to the principal data environment of an enterprise. These data services are available to business applications such as services. Examples of this include applications such as Master Data Management, Business Intelligence, Content Management, Information Integration, and Data Management. Seen from below, Information has its own architecture for the management of the dataflow within the enterprise.

Access

The Access area provides the functionality for the integration of existing legacy application with a SOA. The existing functionality is wrapped up and can thus be reused as a service. In this process, one has to check whether or not the current (legacy) functionality still passes within the semantics of the business model in which it is to be used.

Partner

Partner is comparable to the Interaction area, but is specifically oriented toward providing services to partners, including the control of the interaction with the external party. From a different point of view, Partner and Access can be compared, where specific services are provided by a selected partner. Here, one can think of an external service such as interest calculation of the business processes, which can be an integral component over and above one's 'own' services.

Enterprise Service Bus

The Enterprise Service Bus (ESB) is an essential component within SOA Reference Architecture. This facility supplies functionality such as the routing of messages, translation of various message formats, and the conversion of transport protocols. As a result, it is possible to activate a service via the ESB without knowing the language in which this service was made and where this service runs. At the same time, the ESB ensures the communication between the service consumer and the service provider. Its presence within the SOA Reference Architecture is transparent in relation to the other areas present within the application domain.

The ESB is so important in a SOA environment that it seems that SOA would be impossible without it. But this is not so. Vice versa, people occasionally think that if one has an ESB, one automatically has SOA. That, too, is not true. The two concepts are related and, in the right circumstances, will reinforce one another. But they are not inextricably interconnected.

Business Innovation and Optimization

This area can be used to analyse the business performance and adjust the business design where necessary. A toolset is often used to simulate the effects that certain changes have upon the business design. The results can also be used to implement changes in the business design.

At the same time, it is possible to define Key Performance Indicators (KPIs). These KPIs can be allied to the system environment of the IT Service Management domain so that a direct check can be made or the KPIs activated. This produces new input for possible changes in the business design.

Development

This area is an essential component of any comprehensive integration architecture. The SOA Architecture includes development tools, used to implement custom artefacts that leverage the infrastructure capabilities, and business performance management tools, used to monitor and manage the runtime implementations at both the IT and business process levels.

IT Service Management

Most organizations nowadays use a standardized management process to manage and control their IT environment. The most well-known process is ITIL, which stands for Information Technology Infrastructure Library. It was developed as a reference framework for the layout of an IT organization. It is of great importance that a Service Level Agreement (SLA) is used to ensure good agreements between the customer and the supplier of services. This SLA is an agreement, concluded by the services consumer and the services provider, specifying the services, the quality level, the parties involved, and the circumstances under which the services are provided.

Infrastructure

In this reference model, infrastructure is what we 'traditionally' call infrastructure: hardware, operating systems, storage, etc. As we have seen in the easy concepts of Chapter 3, with SOA, all sorts of services can come to resemble infrastructure, but that's not what is indicated here.

In practice, the focus of SOA lies primarily in the business and information architecture. SOA helps to optimize the flexibility of company processes. However, this flexibility can only be realized if there is an underlying structure that connects seamlessly to the demands posed by a SOA environment. In other words, the business flexibility is very dependent on the flexibility of the IT infrastructure.

A traditional application landscape is often comprised of vertical (monolithic) applications supported by an infrastructure that is application-driven. The diverse IT resources (such as servers and databases) are directly allocated to that specific environment in which unused capacity cannot be assigned to other applications in the near vicinity. This makes operations expensive and changes difficult.

The ideal is a Service Oriented Infrastructure, completely made up of infrastructure services, which comprises a self-regulating, flexible and standardized communications layer that can support the transformation from a vertical application-driven infrastructure to a more horizontal services-driven one.

Architecture that provides a framework for projects

Finally, the type of architecture that serves as a framework for a specific project is more directly concerned with the operational level. Once a positive business case has turned into a project, architecture is required to provide a framework within which design decisions are to be made. The emphasis is on the design: the guidelines and standards with which the project must comply, and also the delineation of projects and any questions concerning reuse that may arise. These architectures provide the degree of precise detail required by the project leader in order to have a sufficient basis on which to make appropriate design decisions for a particular project. This type of architecture is called *Project Start Architecture* (PSA). Every project should get a PSA that prescribes which services should be reused and which services should be developed or adapted. The PSA also contains the service contracts for those services that are involved in the project.

Of course, these types of architecture do not exist separately of each other. In fact, they are different views of the same goal, providing different perspectives on the same circumstances for various purposes and target groups.

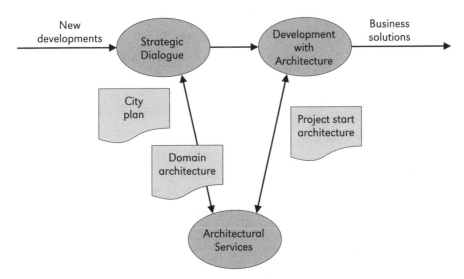

Figure 4.13 Different architecture perspectives

It is important to be aware of the differences in perspective. Being sensitive to the outlook of others increases the chance that the architecture being produced will be practical and well received by people other than those who have formulated it. Avoid the mistake of going into more depth than necessary, as well as the danger of covering too much ground in describing aspects that are irrelevant to the architecture's purpose.

Finally it is important to notice that the more mature your enterprise architecture and governance competencies are, the easier the adoption and implementation of SOA will be. Enhancing your enterprise architecture practice with DYA creates big advantages.

4.8 How to deploy SOA Governance

An organization that manages its Enterprise and IT Governance has a greater chance of success when implementing SOA than an organization where Enterprise and IT Governance is still in its infancy. Setting up SOA Governance is a matter of adapting and enhancing existing Enterprise and IT Governance mechanisms.

On the other hand, SOA can be a catalyst for Enterprise and IT Governance. Because SOA Governance is of paramount importance to successful SOA implementation, it can provide leverage to design and/or improve the Enterprise and IT Governance.

What needs to happen in order to plan Governance? The following three areas are important:
1. The assignment of roles and responsibilities.
2. The design of a management mechanism.
3. The definition of policies.

In the next few sections, we shall discuss these three areas in more detail. It is important to understand, however, that the most important aspect of deploying SOA Governance is to keep it as simple as possible.

Roles and responsibilities

The allocation of roles and responsibilities clearly shows who is responsible for which decisions. In order to know what decisions need to be made, it is important to be clear about the Governance processes. Once the processes themselves are clear, techniques such as RACI and RAEW can be used to determine who has which decision-making authority in these processes. An example of a SOA Governance process could be reviewing services and then assigning authority to a single person or group of people to approve or disapprove of a service design.

RACI and RAEW explained

The letters in RACI stand for:
- (R) Responsible: owner of the project/problem
- (A) Accountable: person with ultimate responsibility/sign-off for the deliverable
- (C) Consulted: has information and/or capability to complete the work
- (I) Informed: the individuals informed but not necessarily consulted

---

In RAEW, the letters stand for:
- (R) Responsibility: the individual supplying the deliverable
- (A) Authority: the person checking and approving the deliverable
- (E) Expertise: the individuals giving advice based on certain expertise
- (W) Work: the persons collaborating in producing the deliverable

Table 4.2 (see page 81) offers a practical aid for the determination of roles and responsibilities in the implementation of SOA. Clarifying these roles and responsibilities is an essential component of setting up SOA Governance. Filling in the table with representatives of all the stakeholders involved in the SOA creates valuable insight into who must do what and who is ultimately responsible.

The tasks mentioned in Table 4.2 are related to the various stages in the life cycle of a service.

Management mechanisms

Control mechanisms are constructs used in the decision-making process. A construction can be a group of people charged with the making of specific decisions, but it can also indicate a method of back-charging or the set-up of a services marketplace. An example of a SOA Governance control mechanism is the adoption of a design authority that is responsible for the monitoring of the correct design and use of services. The design authority has the authority to disapprove of the service design.

Another example of a control mechanism is the service level agreement that indicates the conditions under which the service is delivered.

IT Governance control mechanisms

Many common IT Governance control mechanisms such as the IT Council and Business Process Teams are described in Broadbant and Weil [Broadbent 2002]. In several of Gartner's follow-up publications [Gartner 2006e] these control mechanism are specifically applied to SOA projects. This results in the following constructs:

Executive committee.

Typically enforces decision paths and decides on funding. In SOA, it can also serve as a 'supreme' steering committee to decide issues that the SOA council (see next bullet) can't resolve.

IT Council of business, IT executives.
Discuss funding and enforce the proper involvement of business process owners. When turned into a SOA council, it's the primary place where key SOA Governance decisions (such as 'Is this really a new, reusable service?') are discussed and, in some cases, also made, normally by a restricted subset of participants. When an agreement can't be reached, the council passes on issues to the SOA steering committee.

IT leadership committee.
Supports co-operative working practices across several IT departments. Within SOA, it's essential to foster the developers' buy-in and enforce the new way they're being measured (that is, on reusing established services and developing reusable services, not simply on developing new services).

Enterprise architecture committee.
The center of the Integration Competence Center (ICC) and a major decision center for the SOA.

Business/IT relationship managers.
Fundamental to ensuring business process owners' involvement and fostering agreement on reusable, high granularity services.

Process teams with IT members.
Often already a part of the ICC, even before SOA is discussed. Sometimes it's organized into a process center of excellence, if strong business process management practices are in place. Its work shapes the SOA, especially when it's defined top-down, starting with business processes (which is common in some vertical industries, such as insurance).

Service-level agreements.
They range from the technical quality of service requirements on service response times, to more high-level, reusable service development times for business process owners. Use them extensively.

Chargeback arrangements.
Generally useful to shape behaviour, and to assign and recoup costs. Commonly used in SOA to split the maintenance costs of reusable services among various application owners, proportional to measured service usage by the various applications.

Task	Area of concern	Respon-sible	Account-able	Consulted	Informed
Identification	Global process analysis				
	Global information analysis				
	Formulating a global service description				
	Determination of business domains				
	Contact with (external) businesses that use services				
	Maintaining the service registry				
Specification	Detailed process analysis				
	Performance criteria process				
	Detailed information analysis				
	Formulating a detailed service description				
	Maintaining service registry				
Funding	Funding				
Sourcing/ Planning	Sourcing/Planning				
Development	Service oriented development of systems				
	Maintaining the service registry				
Certification	Certification				
	Maintaining the service registry				
Publication	Maintaining the service registry				
Contracting	Contact with (external) businesses that use services				
	Maintaining the service registry				
Phasing out	Process analysis				
	Information analysis				
	Maintaining the service registry				
Removal	Maintaining the service registry				

Table 4.2 Tool for defining roles and responsibilities with regard to the service life cycle

Policies

Policies are used to prevent uncontrolled growth, and also to ensure efficient working practices such as the reuse of solutions to recurring problems. Policies restrict design freedom and define boundaries. However, by having clearer boundaries, other possibilities become apparent. Policies are reflected in principles, policy directives, standards, and guidelines. They are part of the Enterprise Architecture of an organization. An example of a SOA Governance policy is a set of guidelines for service design.

These activities (defining policies, mechanisms and roles and responsibilities) are interrelated and one can't be done without the other. Installing policies without assigning control mechanisms is not very useful because people don't generally abide by policies. Defining control mechanisms without assigning authority isn't very useful either, as that will only result in a number of chat groups without a clear mandate.

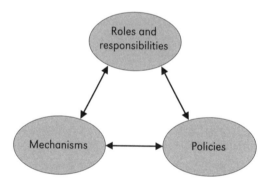

Figure 4.14 Three areas of concern for governance

Control mechanism design and assigning authority are primarily concerned with the management function, the real governance. The definition of policies is primarily a task for Enterprise Architecture. Enterprise Governance and Enterprise Architecture are two sides of the same coin. They need each other. Enterprise Governance without Enterprise Architecture does deliver control mechanisms but without content to manage by. Enterprise Architecture without governance does contain management content but no processes to provide direction.

Organizational structures supporting governance

A way to organize different aspects of SOA is by applying a cross-unit organizational structure which includes the following:

SOA Business Transformation Architecture Council

This team is in charge of gathering the business requirements, performing business domain analysis and process engineering analysis, and identifying the necessary business components, services, and process modules. Instead of following a strict top-down approach, the council should use a mixed approach in blending top-down, bottom-up, and goal-based methods to ensure appropriate services identification. In particular, this team should ensure that the exposed granularity of the defined services matches the business requirements and specifications – matching business components to IT components as services.

SOA Technical Architecture Board

This team ensures the alignment of business and IT, following industry and enterprise standards, and technically ensures that exposed services match the requirements for evolution and reusability, as defined in the general guidelines for enterprise IT development. They are well versed in emerging industry trends, state-of-the-art technologies, and standardization efforts. They are responsible for framing the technical enterprise architecture blueprints (the master IT plan for the enterprise), identifying niche architecture patterns, and promoting reusability principles. They work closely with the SOA transformation team.

Component Design and Development Centers

These are the usual IT teams. They provide design and development of the components and processes, along with new skills such as business process modeling. This team delivers a solution design outline, high and low-level design abstractions, service oriented analysis and design, and various test phases, such as unit, integration, system, acceptance tests.

Operations Center

Finally, there is a production team in charge of the operational aspects of service components. These aspects include managing the quality of service, enforcing business and service level agreements, managing the security context, services chargeback, and revenue assurance. The team is responsible for rolling out the service, performing regular maintenance, and providing overall system management.

All these organizations have to be staffed adequately with people best suited to the newly defined roles in a Service Oriented enterprise. In Chapter 7 on SO people, we will present the new or newly defined roles as required for getting the most benefit from SOA.

A proven institution to obtain SOA Governance in an enterprise is the installation of a SOA Center of Excellence (COE). It is preferably staffed by renowned and recognized leaders on the various disciplines shown in Figure 4.15.

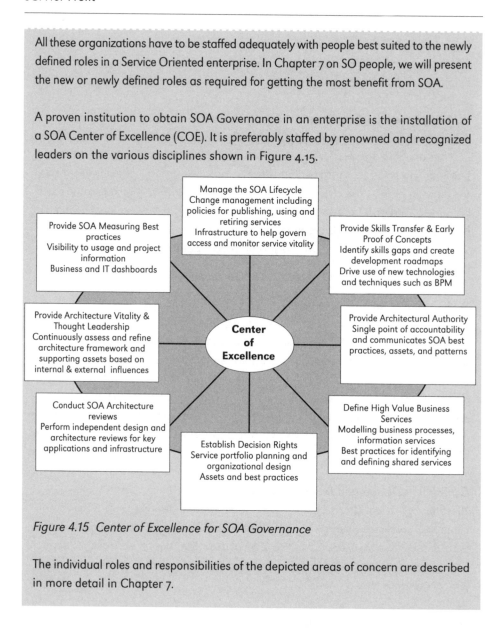

Figure 4.15 Center of Excellence for SOA Governance

The individual roles and responsibilities of the depicted areas of concern are described in more detail in Chapter 7.

Although the importance of governance for SOA is not easily overemphasized, we need to mention that this is not the only success factor in implementing SOA. As we have discussed previously, it is also essential to have a clear vision on the business value and goals of SOA and to have access to the appropriate competences to design, build, implement, and maintain SOAs. Communication and knowledge transfer also require special attention. But in the absence of sound SOA Governance, failure is certain. Timing is of the essence, as the next section discusses.

4.9 How to start with SOA Governance

As mentioned earlier in this chapter, policies and management are absolutely necessary once the going starts to get tough. So should we start to design SOA Governance once things start going wrong? That is not smart. On the other hand, it is not very smart to design a heavy SOA Governance before the first project has even started. Without prior practical SOA knowledge, it appears almost impossible to clearly define all the roles, responsibilities, control mechanisms, and policies in advance. SOA Governance emerges from a learning process where 'just in time' and 'just enough' governance is important. In other words, the design of SOA Governance should run parallel to the adoption and implementation of SOA in the organization. It is important to allow the design of the SOA Governance to run slightly ahead of the need. In other words, rather than react to issues, it should be proactive and anticipate them.

As we mentioned previously, SOA Governance is not a separate sector but rather an integral component of Enterprise Governance. Figure 4.16 shows that the more mature the Enterprise Governance Competency is, the better the chances are for enterprise-wide success with SOA.

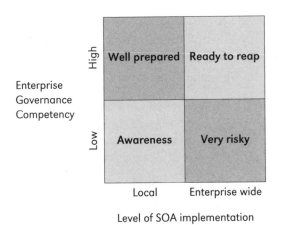

Figure 4.16 Levels of SOA Governance

Figure 4.16 shows that, as the aggregation level at which SOA is implemented increases, it becomes ever more important to have a competent Enterprise Governance function at one's disposal. If the development of this function is a little ahead of the rest, that's no problem. The organization is well prepared to implement SOA throughout the company. The other way around, however – starting on a company-wide implementation of SOA without the proper

Enterprise Governance competency – brings many risks. This means that there is a huge risk of proliferation of services, increased complexity, increased cost of management and maintenance, while the most important promise of SOA – the enhancement of agility and flexibility – cannot be realized.

If SOA is applied with limited scope, it is important to build up knowledge and experience, not only with SOA but also with SOA Governance and thus automatically with Enterprise Governance. At the starting point of SOA, it is essential to give adequate consideration to policies and mechanisms in order to be able to implement SOA successfully. Of course, it remains disputable whether or not it is advisable to apply limited scope SOA to an organization. The only justification lies in the initiation of pilot schemes in order to gain experience. In order to benefit from the business value of SOA, it must be placed in a larger context. Deliberating on Enterprise Governance is a good way to do so. This does not mean, however, that SOA should be implemented immediately and with a big bang. The actual implementation of SOA can best be done gradually in project form, but it must be done within the framework and steering of Enterprise Governance. For this reason it is important to set up the Enterprise Governance in a proactive way.

When applying SOA at enterprise-wide levels, a mature form of Enterprise Governance is needed. If it is not in place, the organization is faced with a challenge, as the Enterprise Governance will have to be set up within or parallel to SOA programmes and projects. This places an extra burden upon the implementation of SOA.

Governance mechanisms

This example describes the way in which a number of governance measures have been taken in the implementation of SOA in an organization that thinks and works with great reliance on the infrastructure. SOA was introduced enterprise-wide in one go, in order to breach the silo forming. This placed heavy demands on SOA Governance.

The starting points for the structuring of SOA Governance were:
- This business does not (yet) think in terms of processes.
- SOA has not (yet) been introduced into the business side.
- There is an Enterprise Architecture (EA) department. This department has knowledge of the organization's business processes and the entire sector.
- Information and service analysis are inextricably linked to process analysis.
- The EA department is the organ where all services are managed.

- The development of services takes place according to the Contract First Principle, in other words, the service contract (service description) is first formulated and then the service is built.

Mechanisms that are set up in the framework of SOA Governance:

Service Project Start Architecture

EA prescribes which services are to be reused for each project, which ones are to be adjusted, and which are to be introduced, with a complete service description on the basis of the Contract First Principle. In other words, a project does not determine what a service will look like. The EA department takes the business process in question and adds the potential of reuse to this (no exhaustive analysis of all possible business processes, but a common sense approach suffices). If the concept of Project Start Architecture already exists, it is supplemented by services.

Budget for commodity services

Without a separate budget for reusable services, an impossible discussion will arise within the organization as soon as a project has to invest in something that can be reused. To stimulate reuse, the business agrees to a budget that is entirely devoted to reuse purposes (commodity services). Ultimately, the service Project Start Architecture is decisive in determining what is a reusable service. Even if there is no budget for commodity services, the Project Start Architecture will ensure the proper service portfolio. Thus, a budget helps, but the Project Start Architecture is decisive. This is immediately the minimum variant in this organization. There are no alternatives because an alternative allows liberties that ensure new silo forming.

Dividing projects

Within this organization, the decision has been taken to separate consumer and provider projects. The consumer project requires certain services: the Project Start Architecture describes which. Then two subprojects are specified: a consumer application project and a provider project. The consumer application project is aimed at delivering a working application. The provider project is aimed at delivering services to the consumer application project. Both projects can be initiated at the same time, in accordance with the Contract First Principle. The budget of the provider comes from the separate budget for commodity services.

This example shows that the organization is in the fortunate circumstance of having EA competency at its disposal. This EA competency is assigned an important role in the framework of SOA Governance.

4.10 Summary

It should be apparent that SOA Governance, and thus Enterprise Governance, is of major importance to the successful implementation of SOA. Without solid governance, the implementation of SOA will fail; there will be little or no chance of reuse and because services are built and bought in different ways, a complex, expensive, and very ineffective IT will be the result.

The implementation of Enterprise Governance is not only a precondition of success for SOA, it also enhances the chance that strategic initiatives will result in successful implementations. Enterprise Governance & Architecture ensure that the changes in an organization occur in a coherent and consistent fashion.

Important areas of SOA Governance are Services Portfolio Management, Services Life Cycle Management and Services Registry. Portfolio Management prevents uncontrolled growth in the services portfolio, Services Life Cycle Management makes sure that services are removed from the services portfolio once they are no longer necessary and a Services Registry makes clear which services are available. The registry is of vital importance for enabling reuse.

Enterprise Architecture is another important area within Enterprise Governance. It is the enterprise architect that has to transcend the boundaries of business units and IT silos to arrive at an optimum set of services for the organization. Dynamic Enterprise Architecture provides a pragmatic model for that purpose. The right SOA-based principles, guidelines and models are created only when there are business objectives which justify the choice for SOA.

The implementation of SOA Governance consists of determining roles and responsibilities, management mechanisms and policies. But above all, SOA Governance is a question of improving the Enterprise Governance and Enterprise Architecture competences. Only when you have a mature form of these competences can you use SOA for profit.

5 Rethink your business

5.1 Introduction

Has your company thought about outsourcing? Or even offshoring? Or how about this: have you thought about outsourcing some of your unit's work to another unit? That's what SOA is about: sharing services across an organization, where it no longer matters where these services reside as long as they deliver the level of service agreed upon. Part of the process that is currently executed within your unit may be taken care of by a service that is provided by another unit, or even externally.

The analogy with outsourcing is valuable for another reason: it shows the level of abstraction you need to apply to your organization to define your SOA correctly. You need to regard reuse and services from a business perspective. You need to see your organization as a network of people and units providing services to each other. You need to find the basic elements that make up your organization. This chapter will show you how to do this in a Service Oriented way.

Thinking about your organization at an abstract level is not rocket science, nor is it new: business optimization has been around for a long time, giving us concepts like shared service centers or staff functions for HR, printing or communications. And, as with other sorts of business optimization, there is value to be found in looking at what other companies have done. Within SOA, this also means looking at the emerging industry models for SOA: ready-made architecture templates defined to fit a certain industry.

To derive the greatest benefit from SOA, your organization should become 'service oriented' at a business level as well. Using SOA in this manner will even enable you to move easily from *business optimization to business model innovation:* finding new ways of applying your capabilities to serve customers.

In this chapter, we shall introduce methods to look at your business in such a way that it becomes easier to spot basic elements and services, and find the value in them. We'll talk about the value of industry models and how they can be used. We'll give you practical tools and examples that will help you speed up the processes of acquiring insight and setting priorities for optimizing your business using Service Oriented Architecture.

5.2 What is your business model?

A business model is an abstract description of your business for a specific purpose. It describes the way you do (or want to do) business. In most businesses there's not just *one* business model that will support all needs, so there's usually a set of different models describing different views. In Enterprise Architecture terms, these different models are grouped under 'business architecture' and ought to be used in both business innovation and IT solution development.

A business model is valuable only when it fits your organization and when it serves a purpose. To find a model with an optimal fit, analysis of the organization is necessary and models of similar companies and industry models can help. To make sure models are usable for transformations, they have to be made from a set of established building blocks that must be designed to last some time, and be immune to change. The configuration of the building blocks may change, due to new processes or products, but the basic elements remain the same. Here we find a great similarity to Service Oriented Architecture itself, in which the services themselves should be rather static, but configurable into many different solutions so as to respond easily to changing circumstances.

The elements in a business model should be described and defined in the same way as 'services' should: independently of each other as much as possible, with clearly defined interfaces, and mirroring how a business really works. Then, the model gains the same benefits as software does with services: the model becomes resilient to change.

To find the business models that fit your organization, you will need to analyse the current situation, analyse the vision and strategy of your organization, and look at existing models and SOA standards. All these combine to form a tailor-made, SOA-based, business model.

Real-world methodology

Throughout this chapter we shall use a global plastic product provider as an example for demonstrating the different models and the relations between them. The examples were distilled from a real life project at this producer during spring of 2006. The examples show what sorts of elements to expect in certain models. The models themselves could of course easily be changed to your industry, whether it's financials, healthcare, or any other industry.

Feedback from the customer

At the start of the transformation project, the method of analysis and business modeling was discussed with the client. Since the industry concerned is very process focused, we were expecting the introduction of this service oriented approach to take a lot of time. To our surprise, the method of modeling (that was very new to this industry) seemed to sell itself: in a round of talks with each director in the group management and other important stakeholders, it took on average only 15 minutes to get a quote like 'that's the right way of looking at our business'.

Other comments were 'This is just common sense, why do it any other way?' and 'We are actually working like this, but current IT application support doesn't reflect it'. In addition to the organizational culture of the company being an important factor, the fact that the model seemed practical and natural was the foundation of this fast adoption.

5.3 From a function to a service oriented organization

Most businesses today are function oriented. Based on theories from Frederich Winslow Taylor (1856-1915) and Luther Gulick (1865-1918) organizations are usually departmental with homogeneous units. These functional organizations with departments and units, as shown in Figure 5.1, were perfectly suitable for a reality where business processes took place locally, at the bottom or end nodes. To optimize this type of organization, all activities performed are analysed and subsequently assigned to a group, without disturbing the homogeneity in each organizational division.

The IT architecture known as 'stovepipe architecture' or 'silo architecture' is the direct result of this structure: there is a unique set of applications supporting each division and each unit, resulting in the present day headache of expensive maintenance and support, and very low agility on a corporate level.

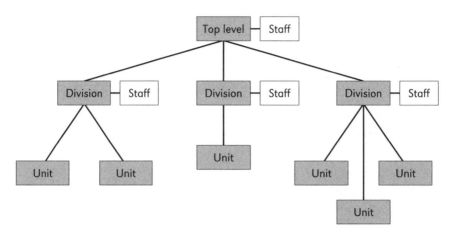

Figure 5.1 Basic functional business model

Time for change

What has been happening for a while, and will continue with higher intensity, is that doing business has become more global, with a higher rate of change. This means, among other things, that the processes initially supported locally are now placed higher up in the model, making them more centralized and more enterprise-wide. There is more focus on sharing applications and processes across organizational units. The basic functional organization models simply don't support the businesses of today, for either private or public organizations.

The service oriented organization

A service oriented organization is an organization based on a common set of business services. The services are linked to business capabilities, which are the high-level things an organization *can* do. The capabilities, then, if needed, are grouped in different business domains that are the largest building blocks for different high-level business models. In order to design solutions, processes are defined with the business services or its abstractions as the building blocks.

The services address the WHAT aspect, the processes address the HOW. One business service can be performed in many capabilities and one capability can be a part of many domains. Figure 5.2 shows a service oriented organization.

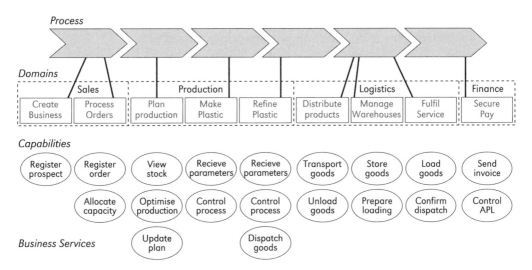

Figure 5.2 Service oriented organization

A business process is executed with help of business services that are contained in business capabilities. The business domains are the organizational entities that perform the business services, with or without IT support.

The map of an entire organization is more complex, of course, with a larger set of processes. Furthermore, business services may support more than one capability (not shown in Figure 5.2). For example the 'View stock' service is used when planning what to produce, but also when deciding where to put the goods in the warehouse.

5.4 The elements of a dynamic business model

The elements that make up a business model need to be fairly stable over time, yet at the same time, the model must describe the business accurately. The levels of abstraction we apply when thinking about an organization are the business domains, the capabilities ('all the things an organization *can* do'), the processes and units, and finally the service lines that ultimately deliver the end-product or service of the organization.

Business domain map
The top level of abstraction is the business domain map. The domains are tailor made to fit the current (and expected) business situations. A domain is

a building block for business models and high-level processes as well as a context/demarcation for an important or prioritized area.

The domains in the map will have different characteristics, such as the organizational units, sub processes, support areas, prioritized areas, or federal control areas. The number of domains to be defined and the number of different characteristics to be used depends wholly on the current organization, its current and potential strategy, and its current business and IT. The example in Figure 5.3 is a simple but common division of domains.

Figure 5.3 Business domain map

Capability map

The domains are basically a sorting structure normally connected to whichever organizational function is performing the business services, 'the WHO'. To get a more action-oriented content in the map, we have to switch to what we call the capability map, 'the high-level WHAT'.

Figure 5.4 Capability map (at an early draft in reality)

Process or unit map

The set of domains or capabilities compiled in a diagram like Figure 5.4 does not add much value in itself. It is just a random collection. It has to be put in a business context to show how the elements provide value. The context could be a process or a unit model.

Figure 5.5 Process context built from domains

The high-level process in Figure 5.5 shows how to put the domains together in a context, a process from sales to receiving pay. The same process built from capabilities is a more action-oriented and prescriptive model, and will look like Figure 5.6.

Figure 5.6 Process context built from capabilities

Service line business model

The process can be even more detailed and practical if connected to a service line, a specific scenario for the delivery of a certain output from the core business process, a service offer.

Thinking of service lines is probably the best way for many organizations to put the capabilities and services into their real business contexts. The domains/capabilities are very suitable as building blocks when describing and building service line flows.

Figure 5.7 describes an example of a service line: 'deliver yoghurt buckets to a high-end customer selling health products, and with a certain delivery Service Level Agreement (SLA)'. The capabilities in the detailed connected process show all important steps required in order to deliver this service offer, the service line. The service line is completed as follows:
1. The service is contracted in Create Business.
2. Delivery orders are received and handled in the Process orders.

3. As the SLA requires products in stock, it has to be production-planned for these certain circumstances.
4. The first production step is to produce the base plastic.
5. The second step is Refine the plastic by form pressing it into buckets and adding a printable surface, all according to the contracted product specification.
6. The buckets are distributed to a warehouse close to the customer in order to secure the SLA.
7. The buckets are delivered from the warehouse to the customers printing partner on demand according to the SLA.
8. The service provider gets paid according to the delivery result and contracted circumstances.
9. The delivery case is ended after quality follow-up and eventual claims handling.

Figure 5.7 Service line business model

During the complete process both strategic KPIs are controlled and the Delivery Process is monitored.

Down at this detail level, we are at the lowest level of business models based on processes, something we can call the Service Line Business Model.

The basic elements in these diagrams (capabilities and services) can be used to define all sorts of models, such as looking at the business along other lines than that of 'process', for instance. At this stage, the business model is still only a foundation. When implementing a solution, the process will be a lot more detailed, although still fully based on this foundation.

5.5 How to find the elements of your dynamic business model

We have seen the elements that can be used to make a dynamic business model, and the maps we can create. So how do you find the specific elements that make up the models of your organization, and can you rethink your business using these models?

First of all, you need to get insight into the business strategy that will help build a picture of the (near) future, find the non-changing parts of the organization, and separate them from the changing parts. The business needs to respond to change, the models need to facilitate this change, and the rate of change to expect should be defined by the strategy (which, in turn, is derived from the long-term business vision).

Next, there are a few views of the organization that will help identify the SOA building blocks as well as fuel the rethinking process. These views are:
- Value chains.
- Connected processes.
- Strategy cascades.

These views are useful to enable discussion because they are based on business and strategy in reality and they are at the right level of abstraction. Experience shows that defining the different modeling components and their demarcations is a matter of time and commitment. How much time largely depends on how quickly you understand and accept the modeling idea. It will take less time if the views described here are used in a structured manner. The views will also ensure the right level of abstraction. Using the right level of abstraction helps to avoid excessively detailed and endless discussions. Sticking to the right abstraction level is a key success factor in creating the basic elements for business modeling.

After looking at the organization using the views mentioned, you can draw up a *capability map* (the most valuable model for SOA) and define the *services*.

Follow the value chain
The value chain is the first enabling view to be used. Discussions about the value chain will help identifying the key areas and aspects of the business.

Figure 5.8 shows a common value chain. It shows the basic capabilities (or domains) upon which the core business process is built, and how it interacts with management and support processes.

Figure 5.8 *Value chain with surrounding key areas*

When discussing the value chain, different ways to deliver the products may become clear. It's a valuable exercise to define a business model like the one below. Figure 5.9 shows a business where there are two key flows of product delivery: goods and services.

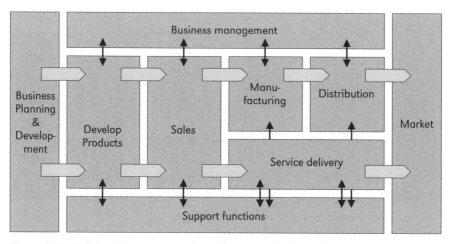

Figure 5.9 *High-level business model with the key business domains*

This is common in many businesses, and in some cases it is obvious that goods and pure services can't be handled the same way. Many companies have fallen into the trap of using a system designed for *goods* to take care of the *service-*based products. The result of this kind of combination is usually a tattered standard business solution. Another trap, which can be avoided by using the model above, is that new standard solutions bought for a specific domain tend to extend its functionality beyond the defined boundaries.

A business model on this level is valuable if it reflects the federal domains as well as the different key service lines. The value derived from this model is that it can be used as a pattern for the demarcation and standardization of IT system domains.

Look at connected processes

At this stage, when the highest business abstractions have been discussed and defined, it's time to get into a more practical view of the business. The natural next step is to use the aspect of connected processes. The starting point is the value chain.

The discussions should focus on the connected processes used or needed to fulfil the business process on a more detailed level. The result from the exercise is a map as in Figure 5.10.

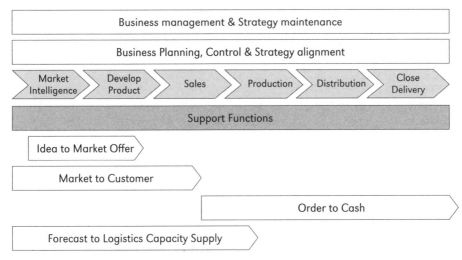

Figure 5.10 Connected processes

The block arrows show the key connected processes in the business, positioned in relation to the value chain. While working with the different models above, the capability map should be successively revised and updated.

Down a strategy cascade

When analysing the organization, another constructive view is to take the business strategy as the leading aspect. You can then look at how the strategy is implemented in the organization. Which actions do the units take to follow the strategy, how do the combined activities support the strategy? This will help you find the parts of the organization that are of strategic importance (which unit really contributes to the strategy, and which units hardly have any link to the strategy at all?). This view will also give you insight into the way strategy (and innovation) is managed in your organization. Is the definition of strategy an ongoing process, or is it redefined once every three years? Is strategy explicitly part of your governance structure?

Make a capability map

After using these views, the final product from the modeling sessions is, besides the models themselves, the real SOA modeling foundation, the capability map.

Figure 5.11 Set of capabilities, a capability map

As different views have been used and discussed, the capability map is more or less validated at this stage. To develop and validate the capability map further, each connected process that has been identified can be designed with help from the defined capabilities. If a capability is missing, this will be obvious when designing the connected processes. Figure 5.12 is an example of a connected process.

Figure 5.12 Connected process built from pre-defined capabilities

The process has been built from pre-defined capabilities. If taken to this level, the capability map will be quite well validated, especially if also future scenarios have been discussed and defined.

Services

The final step to be executed in this SOA foundation building process is to run through all capabilities and identify which services are needed to fulfil their main tasks. The capabilities are populated with the business services needed to fulfil each capability, as shown in Figure 5.13.

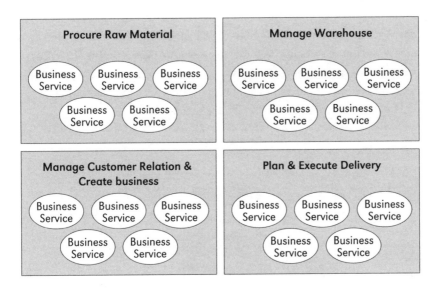

Figure 5.13 Selected set of capabilities populated with services

At this step you also describe the key information flows, with at least flows in and out from a capability point of view. Ideally you define information flows in and out for each business service but if there's little time, you can do it for the most important services only.

In a world of services

When the business services have been defined, put in capability context, and the high-level properties for each capability have been defined, the foundation for any business modeling and process implementation is in place. With the elements described so far, you can model your business and optimize it to fit a dynamic and competitive world.

A true service oriented organization has defined building blocks (Services and/or Capabilities) that can be used to create new service assortment and service lines. Tools are used for assembling the processes to sell and deliver the service assortment, as well as for the simulation of feasibility and business value. The building blocks themselves are SOA components enabled by IT, which speeds up the process to add or change both applications and service lines.

Another method for strategic business transformation: IBM's Component Business Modeling

IBM's Component Business Modeling (CBM)™ is a method that can also be used to design a current and future state business architecture [IBM Global Business Services 2006c]. In CBM, business activities are grouped in autonomous business components. The business components are defined as 'a part of an enterprise that contain similar activities and have the potential to operate independently'.

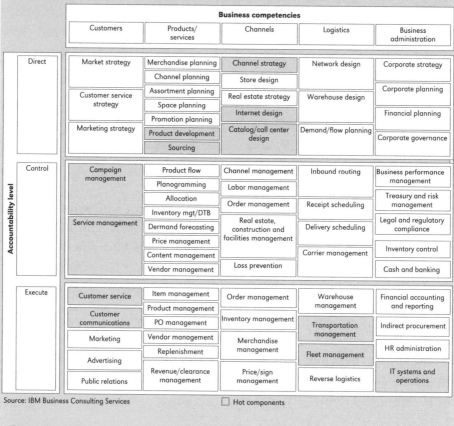

Figure 5.14 Component business map

The method provides organizational mapping and prioritization using models, as in Figure 5.14.

Each business component is defined by describing five dimensions of the component, as depicted in Figure 5.15.

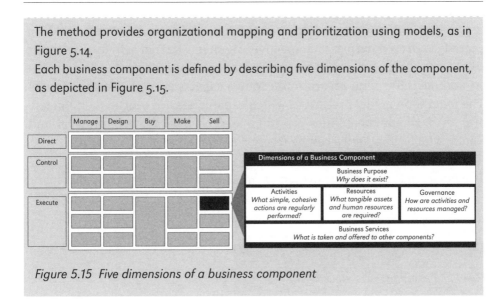

Figure 5.15 Five dimensions of a business component

5.6 From silo to shared

Thinking about your business will bring up the matter of silos in the organization: siloed organizational units (several units may be performing the same activity, but are not willing to abandon the activity) and IT application silos.

Siloed applications exist because organizational units had the freedom to create them: to make applications that were specifically suited for their needs without caring about other parts of the organization. The main characteristics of the old architecture are:

- Each unit has its own application map.
- The level of standardization is low.
- The flexibility for change is low.
- The possibility to create integrated solutions quickly is hampered.

SOA will break the silos down, and replace them with a mixed model: lots of important services will be shared across the organization and a few services will be specific to the business unit in question.

What is central, and what isn't?
The decision to define certain capabilities as 'central' or shared has an immediate impact on the freedom of the units in an organization.

It is important to define which capabilities are common and federal (or shared) from an enterprise perspective. Another essential activity is to define what is standard and what is free choice at local level. The result from analysis and decisions with regard to these two aspects is the Federation model. The federation model prescribes which capabilities are executed on the federal level, which capabilities are to be steered from the federal level and, finally, which capabilities can be freely determined at local unit level.

The model in Figure 5.16 shows an example of capabilities that are on federal level.

Figure 5.16 Federal capability map

At a unit level, the two standards coincide: the federal and the local standard. The capability map at unit level can be used to distinguish which capability is to be provided locally, and which is a shared one. This map can then be used to plan the future application map.

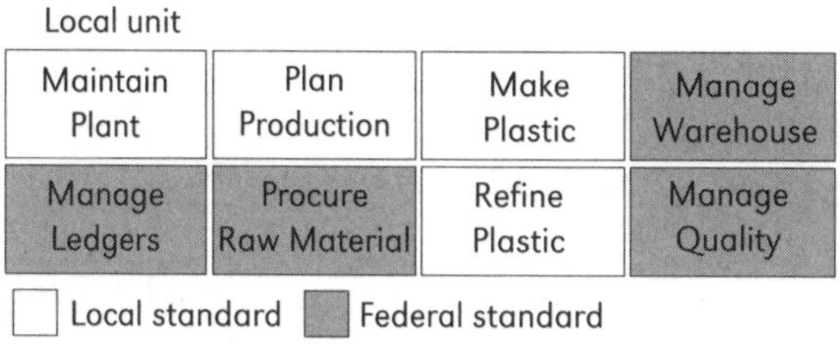

Figure 5.17 Local federation model

Federal standards are defined at enterprise level and the goal is that each capability ought to be supported by only one application throughout the enterprise. For the local standard, each unit has the freedom to select a solution as long as it sticks to capability demarcations, and implements the standard integration interfaces (other architectural restrictions might apply, such as platform preferences and vendor selection).

Federation models with explicit interfaces help steer an organization along the transformation road where the organization discards all bad characteristics of the old architecture.

From model to software

If we take one of the capabilities from the previous picture, we can draw a more detailed diagram, as shown in Figure 5.18. This more detailed diagram can then be used directly to select or define an IT solution. If, for example, a solution for Manage Warehouses has to be procured, the detailed capability model with its population of Business services will act as a high-level functional requirements specification. The model, including the information flows in and out from the capability, sets the requirements for integration. In this specific case, it may be enough from a functional point of view to send for vendors that might supply a ready-made solution.

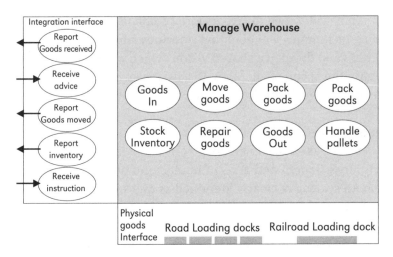

Figure 5.18 Populated capability model for a selected capability

From this simple view, with the addition of specific business rules and technology requirements like a web service-based integration interface, any Warehouse Management System vendor can create a basic offer and specification for a solution.

5.7 How to set priorities

You can't start changing everything at the same time. The SOA maturity model will help you select aspects of your business and IT operation that need optimizing. At the same time, you will also need to select the business parts that need optimization most urgently: begin with the parts whose improvement makes the most sense businesswise. To find these business priorities, you can use several techniques, of which we list a few:

- The Benefit/Ease matrix.
  Looking at investments and returns for each domain and capability.
- Domain and capability prioritization.
  Finding consensus among stakeholders on the most important capabilities or domains to address first.
- Value chain analysis.
  Finding consensus along the lines of the value chain.
- Strategy cascade.
  Deriving priorities directly from the overall business strategy.

Most techniques can be combined to give a more complete view of priorities. Consensus building techniques will help find priorities and at the same time help build awareness and develop a shared vision, which will help the introduction and increase the speed of adoption. Discussions will arise, highlighting critical points in your business architecture.

The Benefit/Ease matrix
The Benefit/Ease matrix, as shown in Figure 5.19, is a tool for defining a solution or an opportunity's Benefit and Ease of implementation. The ones with highest score on both scales are clearly identified as quick hits and potential starters of a transformation.

The matrix is useful for common fast prioritizations within a group. The facilitator runs through a selected set of capabilities. The group has to reach consensus on where to place the capabilities in the matrix. It is good to document the conditions behind the positioning. Usually, each object that is mapped into the matrix enables a valuable discussion. It may be difficult for participants to understand the scale on the axis. In order to deal with this, an initial exercise to create understanding of the axis and the scale values can be performed.

When the mapping session is over, the quick hits identified are the capabilities closest to the upper right-hand corner of the matrix.

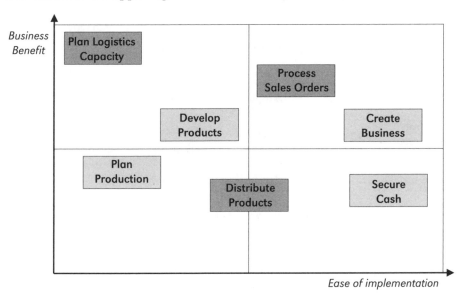

Figure 5.19 Benefit/Ease matrix

Domain/capability prioritization

Domain/capability prioritization is a technique used to find out which capabilities in the capability map ought to be prioritized. It is normally suitable to look from two main perspectives: opportunities and issues.

The main stakeholders are invited to vote in a workshop or through interviews; first, on which capabilities they think have the best improvement potential (opportunities), and second, on which capabilities have the largest problems (issues). The result is compiled into the capability map or any other representation based on the capabilities in Figure 5.20.

After the voting, it is good to run through the result and discuss the reasons behind the voting. A documentation of the reasons is a good complement to the prioritized map above.

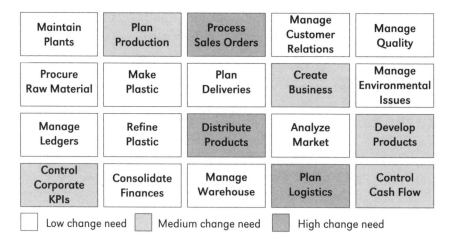

Figure 5.20 *Capability map with change priorities indicated by colour*

Value chain analysis

Despite its simple shape, the value chain is a quite good platform for business prioritization work. It is suitable for initial workshop activities and quick analysis. Where are the issues? Where are the opportunities? The same voting exercise as mentioned in the domain/capability prioritization can be applied to the value chain and its steps. To do the prioritization in more detail, each step in the chain needs to have its capabilities attached. The prioritization is then done at capability level. The value chain can be used to summarize the result whatever the detailed level of work.

Figure 5.21 shows an example from a global consumer product manufacturer a few years ago. The summary from the analysis done on subprocess level was presented from a value chain point of view. In this case, the procedures around distribution are perceived to be the most urgent for change. In the transformation plan the area of distribution was given the highest priority. In practice extra attention was paid to better integration of services and changes in responsibilities. The latter was possible due to the implementation of a portal solution, thus decoupling the IT-supported tasks from the organization.

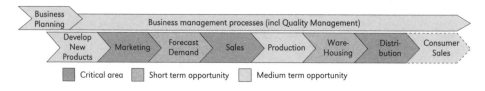

Figure 5.21 *Value chain with urgency levels*

Strategy cascade

Another way of penetrating different aspects to support prioritization is the use of a Strategy cascade. A strategy cascade means that each key strategy area is analysed. Typical areas could be Cost superiority, Differentiation and Quality. The cascade can be done on domains, connected processes or steps in the value chain. If you consider a connected process such as the analysis object, the cascading question could be something like: 'how can we achieve cost superiority in the process to secure capacity supply from forecasts?'. These questions are answered for all objects per strategy area. The result will be a large set of opportunities based on the actual business strategy. They will be on very different levels, so extra work needs to be done to group and re-interpret them, and transform them into useful input for the transformation plans.

Workshop template: *Spotting SOA opportunities*

This template outlines a mini-project that will get you underway in setting up a SOA Transformation plan. In less than three weeks, you will gain valuable insight into priorities and vision by performing a series of interviews and holding a workshop to align all parties. The idea of the visioning process methodology described here is to quickly identify and evaluate the business potential for a specific IT development. 'Cut through the hype and grasp the real potential of SOA' is the slogan today. As IT is both business-driven and a driver for business innovation, the target audience for the visioning process is the management team and other key business leaders, ideally 8-10 people. In this mini-project, some of techniques discussed in this chapter are used.

The process is very quick and, in all cases, generates amazingly interesting and valuable results. The visioning methodology can be seen as a fast rethinking process.

In three weeks calendar time and one-and-a-half day participation per contributor, you will achieve the following:

- Defined, prioritized and established SOA business opportunities.
- Management consensus and understanding of SOA and its potential.
- Management consensus and understanding of other aspects of the business.
- New angles on the business strategy, and maybe a foundation for a change of strategy.
- A foundation for building the first draft of a high-level SOA Transformation plan.

The methodology contains four parts:

1 Focus interviews.
2 Analysis and workshop preparations.
3 Workshop.
4 Documentation and follow-up.

1. Focus interviews

Focus interviews give a well-founded view of the strategy, plans, and expectations from a group of stakeholders. The interviews are performed individually with all participants. A well-prepared interview template is used in all interviews. The battery of questions and exercises scrutinizes the business's and the individual's thoughts from many angles. The target audience consists of the management team and other key business leaders, ideally 8-10 people. The purpose of the interview is to get an overall picture of strategy and priorities as a basis for a workshop. The expected time needed per interview is 2 hours.

Example of an interview template:
- Introduction: The high level objective of the transformation plan is described and individual expectations are gathered.
- What trends are you aware of for your industry segment? Are they perceived as carriers or barriers?
- In a longer perspective (>5 years), how would you describe the organization's goal and visions?
- What are the main challenges facing your company in the next five years?
- What are your companies most prioritized customer segments?
- What distribution channels do you use to reach these segments?
- What are the five most important advantages you strive to give your main customers?
- Who are your competitors and why?
- What are your strengths? (state three)
- What are your greatest opportunities? (state three)
- Discussion: A hypothetical value chain is discussed and change proposals documented.
- Discussion: The capability model is discussed and the key information flows and human interaction points from the actual individual point of view are identified.
- What is your perception of current IT support, what is good and what is bad?
- What is your perception of IT in terms of maturity, your own and the organization as a whole?
- Prioritizing: A card sorting session is performed, aiming to identify and prioritize opportunity areas. Ideally the cards are the same as the blocks in the capability model. The participant has to select a maximum of five cards (areas) which he thinks have the greatest opportunity, and then rank them mutually. The reason for the selection is discussed and documented.
- Do you know which IT applications your competitors have, and is there any IT application you wish you had?
- Finally, do you have any advice for our forthcoming work?

2. Analysis and workshop preparations

The results from the interviews are compiled into a summary, a common draft of the value chain and domain/capability model is created, and the common result of the opportunity prioritization is compiled.

Based on the ideas gathered from best practices, research is performed to identify and describe the organization's best practices. Other SOA best practices applicable to the current business, which are known to or identified by the visioning facilitator's team, are also collected and defined.

The workshop is very carefully prepared, to ensure there are no disturbances during the workshop. Since the time reserved for the workshop is short, there little room for unexpected interruption. Preparation for the workshop consists of planning the brainstorming sessions and prioritization, as well as identifying possible interferences in advance.

3. The workshop

The workshop will start communication, build consensus, and give a common view on the opportunities and the road ahead. The workshop is a full-day session where the brainstorming usually takes place after lunch.

Example of a workshop agenda template:

- Presentation of the results from the interviews: 'Your common view' (by means of a presentation with open, moderated discussions).
- 'The art of possibility', examples and best practices of SOA are presented. Preferably in order of zooming in on the organization: worldwide practices, industry practices, and finally the industry segment. Starting off with a demystifying explanatory discussion to clear up any existing questions (by means of a presentation) is an option.
- Brainstorming session: What are your opportunities with SOA? (by moderated brainstorming)
- Sorting into opportunity areas (by moderation technique).
- Prioritization based on a Benefit/Ease matrix (by discussion/voting).
- If time allows: A strategy cascade for the highest prioritized opportunities (by structured brainstorming).
- If time allows: An action plan is set (by discussion).

4. Documentation and follow up

The results of the interviews and workshop are documented and used to draw models that can be used in a SOA transformation plan. Once momentum has been created, extra care is taken to use this momentum when setting the next steps along the SOA journey.

5.8 How industry models will help you along

To look into the value of industry models, to speed up the process, think about this: What's specific about your company? What distinguishes you from your rival? And what's just 'plumbing'? Wouldn't it be great if, for all the 'plumbing', there was a simple ready-made plan that details all services, capabilities, and processes? And maybe also ready-made IT solutions that support these processes? Well, there is, and there are, sort of.

Industry models are emerging, describing the common elements across an industry. Like a common data model describing products and services, industry models now describe processes, capabilities, and services. If an industry model exists for the industry your company is in, actually looking at it, or getting involved in shaping it, might give you a headstart for modeling and optimizing your business on the 'plumbing' part. For example, there are some ready-made capability maps out on the market. IBM's CBM, Component Business Modeling, has good support for round-trip engineering (linking business modeling directly to the production of software). CBM has direct connections to a large set of ready-made full process designs that can be implemented quickly as solutions.

For the things that make your company unique, there's less help. Sometimes your business uses a radically different model than most competitors, and a business model from a different industry might help but, most often, it's up to the company to define its own.

The golden rule should be: reuse all you can, without relinquishing your competitive advantage. And when looking for reusable elements, you don't have only to look for entire models, you can also look at specific solutions for the silo/shared challenge, for example, or for a specific capability that is a major challenge for your company to execute.

5.9 Summary

In this chapter, we introduced a new way of looking at your business: a top-down way of looking at the domains, services, and capabilities that make up your organization. This new way of modeling will also enable a new way of thinking about an organization, allowing a transformation from a functional to a service oriented organization that will be easier to change and be more focused on the things that distinguish your company from its competitors.

We have shown that it is fairly easy to get down to the level of services in a few steps that get more detailed every time. We have also described different aspects of a transformation from the functional organization and its 'silo'-oriented architecture to a service oriented organization and architecture. The transformation is the final result of the process of rethinking the business.

Finally, we have given you practical tools to start a discussion and set priorities for change.

6 Service oriented organization

6.1 Introduction

In the chapter entitled 'Rethink your business' we discussed how enterprises traditionally organized along business lines are confronted with difficulties in today's ever-changing world. When this rate of change is further increased by the modern means of communication flattening the world, it becomes clear why the philosophy and objectives of SOA challenge you to rethink your business.

In this chapter we will show how the SOA principles can be applied to an organization itself. We will show how business units, teams and people can also be seen as services, and how this enables a truly dynamic organization. For this we introduce the concept of the Human Services Bus. While we do not expect you to reorder your organization to fully embrace this concept, reading about it will help you rethink your business, and help you see the changes that are ahead when SOA will be the standard architecture model.

6.2 An example

Imagine the following situation. In the 1980s/1990s, as one of the first mobile phone providers, you developed a business model based on the demands of early mobile phone customers. On this basis, you established the infrastructure and an organization with all the necessary business units. The company could cover all identified needs of these early users most efficiently. A network of switches and networks was installed all over the country, through which you were able to offer the best prices for regular calls from almost everywhere in your region. This capability allowed your company to grow and become the leading mobile provider.

Your enterprise is organized along the necessary business units and each has its own designated IT department caring for best performing solutions in support of each business unit. As a result, each of the business units gets optimized and utilizes the most efficiently operating solutions that support these dedicated tasks, e.g., billing, customer order entries, or switch operations.

Now, after some time, competitors start to enter your market. One competitor offers flat rate contracts to the customers while calling in specific locations, and another competitor provides excellent call center services, which allow the customer to ask for the most suitable contract based on his individual call history. In order to match these new offers and stay competitive, you analyse your current structure only to find that any of these new offers requires you to change your underlying IT solutions across the board. The structure that was once so successful in building up the business now suddenly becomes a liability to the company's survival.

As discussed previously, SOA can be of help in this situation. It offers individual well-defined services for the required new task or changed processes, taking the results from several of the business units' data services and combining them into a new service for your customers. You might consider implementing the what-if service on tariffs and customer usage patterns as an information service. So far, a technical solution might help.

But now your call center agent must be empowered to change the calling customer from rate A to rate B quickly, just overriding several settings and in fact creating a new contract between your company and the customer. And this should be possible on the fly, without interference and without lengthy request processes involving several lines of business decision. In the situation where a customer wants to get a flat rate for a certain region, there has to be a way to invoke all appropriate services in order to satisfy the customer and arrange a set of services. The customer has to be located and charged according the new tariff conditions.

The example clearly shows that after installing a service-based solution, a need emerges for an adequate organization. Although SOA provides a most flexible platform for the IT system, the challenge for the enterprise is to adapt its structure accordingly in order to fully realize the potential of service orientation. In the case of the example given, this means empowering the individual and providing a service-operation rules base that assures business agility as demanded by the customers.

6.3 **Loosely coupled but well governed**

Hierarchical structures along the lines of business (the silos in the enterprise) are no longer efficient enough for quick reactions to the constantly changing requirements to which a business has to respond.

The adoption of SOA therefore is an inspiration to experiment and migrate to new organizational models that are intended to establish a service oriented enterprise. Some characteristics of this type of enterprise are mentioned below.

> **Challenges by SOA to enterprise organization**
> * Breaking silos is mandatory.
> * Flexibility is created by structuring around processes and business needs.
> * Need of a service oriented organization in a service oriented enterprise.
> * SOA brings the business to IT and vice versa.
> * Business goals based on customer demands determine the action.
> * Dialogue about services that aligns business with IT.
> * SOA aligns business & IT strategies.

The first challenge one faces when organizing the enterprise for the best utilization of a service oriented infrastructure is to break down the silos, i.e., organize across traditional business unit boundaries. It turns out that individuals find it easy to work across boundaries: email, collaboration portals and instant messaging allow them to share information. This can be *ad hoc*, well planned, synchronous or asynchronous: one can structure work around the business processes and needs.

It is important that processes, such as those initiated by customer demand, are executed along certain rules, passing various business units and finally delivering the expected results. The processes can be fully planned or just initiated by individuals according to accepted guidelines, but any unproductive involvement of non-contributors, such as asking a manager whether another unit can be involved, or 'inventing' decisions on-the-fly by management when the assigned employee refuses to take responsibility, should be avoided.

The set of collaborative tools, such as email, shared databases, instant messaging, integrated VoIP solutions, access to IT and business services, can be regarded as the backbone, the mediation tools for humans who co-operate. This is similar to how an enterprise service bus mediates at a technical level. Finally, this could change how people work to serve their customer needs, because it empowers them to find each other in order to fulfil the required tasks. This type of innovative organization model is the so-called 'Human Services Bus' [Bieberstein 2006].

6.4 The Human Services Bus

An organization using a model like the Human Services Bus (HSB) derives its structure by extending traditional SOA semantics and factoring existing organizational structures – blending them to maximize advantages and reduce limitations.

6.4.1 The Collaboration and Orchestration Bus (COB)

In its core, the HSB is comprised of a communication and collaboration framework that is the IT engine to support the HSB logical structure. Analogous to way in which the Enterprise Services Bus connects the services in a SOA, the Collaboration and Orchestration Bus (COB) connects people in their individual roles in the enterprise.

One can imagine this as SOA reference architecture filled by humans instead of programmed services. In an enterprise, the employees, business partners, and customers are service requestors and service providers.

The COB provides the IT infrastructure to formally advertise the team services, offering workflow tools to support joint activities and coordination across services (and teams), task completion monitoring, and early crisis detection. The Service Agents on each layer are supplied with specific planning and design tools to discover, orchestrate and choreograph niche services from the lower service layers. Executive dashboards and configurable reporting tools provide just-in-time snapshots of various service flow metrics and productivity data.

The services are virtualized, and the individuals on the teams supporting the particular service could be geographically dispersed. To support teaming, the COB also provides a portfolio of collaboration tools. A comprehensive array of synchronous and asynchronous tools forms the COB messaging backplane. Facilities like e-meetings with electronic whiteboards, instant messaging, webcasts, and task-oriented community tools supplement the existing synchronous communication facilities, such as teleconferences. With the advent of Web 2.0, which is gaining ground in enterprises today, even more means will become available.

In Figure 6.1, the organization around the COB is shown in more detail. Directory tools that help to find best-fitting individuals, assets and services offered are important for enabling people to work co-operatively in the HSB, so that customer demands can be fulfilled. Service orchestrating and monitoring tasks are supported by the appropriate tools in order to help management arrange the identified and available services successfully. In the end, the result is the requested service to the customer.

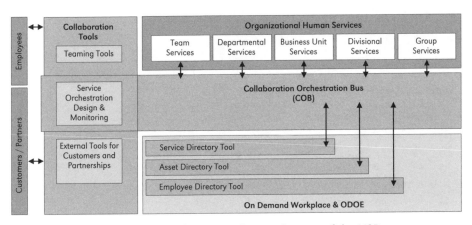

Figure 6.1 Collaboration and Orchestration Bus as the core of the HSB

6.4.2 Defining the Service Structure

One can simply install the COB, or only elements like email or a shared database and leave it to the employees to use it. This certainly might work out fine in small or medium-size organizations, but a certain organizational structure should be established in large enterprises or units. This is surely a governance issue and entails an organizational element.

The following outline presents an abstract description of how the Human Services Bus can be set up. The central logical entity in the HSB is the service. Services can be anything that is considered to execute a particular task –

delivering objectives, tactical results, or strategy realization. Services can further be aggregated to create larger, complex services.

Figure 6.2 depicts the various service layers within an HSB and their *raison d'être*. Additionally, to get the services to perform optimally and to streamline the operative aspects, *Service Agents* need to be defined. These are individuals who are responsible for monitoring, mediating in, or choreographing these services. Their roles and responsibilities vary, depending on the layer, and are critical to the HSB.

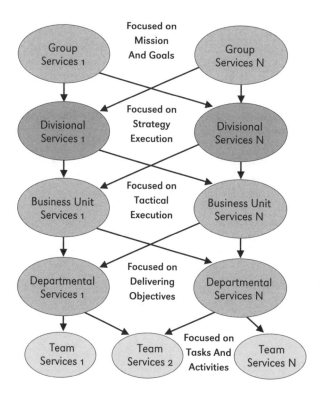

Figure 6.2 Human Services Bus as part of the Operational Network

Team Services

These are the most fundamental services within the HSB. These services are clearly defined to deliver tasks and perform activities relating to the organization's core competencies. The skills of the team services would be niche and precise, such as, 'Functional Testing of Component A in Product XYZ', 'Data Access Performance Benchmarking in Retail Industry', and 'Level 1 Customer Support for Component B in product XYZ'. The Service Agent for this layer is a manager whose responsibility is to 'mediate' and ensure that the service is operational and meets contractual obligations, to optimize the links to the collaboration engine, to troubleshoot day-to-day issues, and to handle team incentives and morale regularly.

Departmental Services
The team services are aggregated at departmental level to deliver core business objectives in order to create Departmental Services such as 'Testing Component A in Product XYZ', 'Performance Benchmarking in Retail Industry', and 'Customer Support on Component B in product XYZ'. Senior Managers are the first-level Service Choreographers – they are responsible for understanding the business objectives delegated to them. They create a service workflow based on the existing services in order to satisfy that objective and ensure that the workflow connections are streamlined by liaising with Team Service Managers.

Business Unit Services
These services are created by choreographing the departmental services to execute the tactical goals of the company. Examples would be 'Testing of Product XYZ', 'Industry Performance Benchmarking', and 'Customer Support of Product XYZ'. The Business Unit Services can also supplement the departmental services orchestration by leveraging the Team Services directly to meet some of their key requirements. It takes executive skills to craft the business unit services that execute and deliver the tactical elements and manage key profit and loss results. A Director is responsible for choreographing the departmental and team level services to meet these needs. He teams up with the Service Agents in the layers below to evaluate the services which his unit uses. He locates process bottlenecks, reengineers the service characteristics when needed, eliminates service redundancies, and defines new 'emerging' services.

Divisional Services
Business unit services need to be threaded to drive the organization's strategic objectives. The Divisional Services can be 'Manage Product XYZ', 'Manage Industry Solutions', 'Customer Relations', etc. The divisional services have the gamut of team, departmental and divisional services at their disposal and can leverage them at their optimal granularity. Senior level executives, such as Vice Presidents and General Managers, are responsible for realizing the strategic objective by orchestrating the Divisional Services and optimally channelling the funds.

Group Services

These services are completely focused on executing the overall mission and goals of the organization. They define the strategies and manage them by orchestrating the divisional services. Examples could be 'Software Portfolio Services', 'Industry Solutions Services', etc. Senior Vice Presidents (SVP) work with the CEO and his corporate team to specify the periodic goals and set the overall organization strategy. Each SVP monitors the efficiency and results of his divisional and business unit services and creates directives to achieve those goals.

The size of the teams representing the services depends on the activity, scope and sizing. Certain team services that have a high demand (e.g. 'Administrative / Secretarial Services') can have replicated services supported by multiple service teams. The density required for a particular service will be driven by the business needs and the costs.

Defining services with differentiated activities and distinct results will help streamline a large organization and remove redundant teams and reduce expenses. It will also facilitate the services discrimination – helping eliminate less strategic services and creating new services with 'emerging' needs. This agility will make the organization adapt quickly to new opportunities and competitive threats. Both the IT-centric and human-centric services are externalized in the same manner, and the service contract defined by the interface abstracts the origin of the service.

6.5 The significance of Web 2.0 to a service oriented enterprise

Agile Business from flexible IT demands Enterprise Business Transformation
- Re-organizing the IT landscape for more flexible operations.
- Re-organizing enterprise structures towards requested agile operations.
- The How-to-Make an 'agile enterprise' operational.
- Tools and IT are just the means not the drivers of the operation.
- Business needs and goals as primary driver.
- Measuring business success per individual service.
- Organization matching needs for empowered professionals.
- Guidelines and organizational structures that support a service oriented enterprise.

As summarized in the frame above, the tools to design the services or the business processes consisting of well-defined and orchestrated services are available for expert use and reuse. Besides the planned, pre-planned and prepared services, there are increasing quantities of tools available to the individual professional who modifies and creates certain services and tools in a more *ad hoc* style. Such individual tools are becoming widely available in the wake of Web 2.0 developments.

Asynchronous communication is supported by specialized team rooms, project databases, interactive team portals and forums, and email. More than that, Web 2.0 provides tools within easy access of each person taking part in the HSB model for arranging one's workplace and for creating useful *ad hoc* tools suited to the individual business situation. Table 6.1 presents an overview of the various concepts that are part of Web 2.0.

Technology	Definition of tasks and usage
Social networks	Technology to leverage personal connections
RSS	A standard for users to collect and read contents feed
Open Source Software	Publicly available software
Blogs	Online diaries containing text, pictures, and other electronic media items
Search engines	Publicly available to find web contents
User review portals	Portals allowing peer review on services or products
P2P file sharing	Sharing media files in online communities
C2C eCommerce	Platform to trade items online
Comparison shopping sites	Sites allowing consumers to compare prizes for products and service offerings
Podcasts	Online video or audio for download to repetitive consummation
Wikis and other collaborative tools	Shared publishing on the internet
Tagging	Meta data assigned to items on the internet

Table 6.1 Web 2.0 concepts

Most of the technologies listed in Table 6.1 may be consumed as services by every employee in the organization. However, depending on the know-how of the individuals concerned, their self-generated tools become more or less sophisticated, and are offered to their peers. To a certain degree, even a specific market can grow within an enterprise, which means software solutions are being provided and deployed independently of the central IT shop.

The task of the central IT department is now to provide the appropriate platform and monitor the ongoing actions on the net, in order to avoid abusive or illegal actions. As a manager's job becomes one involving rule definition and monitoring, the central IT turns into a service provider of infrastructure, IT services, and a measuring unit. More details on the roles and the implications on the individuals are discussed in Chapter 7, Service Oriented People. In the interest of flexibility and agile operation in the enterprise, it is desirable to allow this platform to grow freely. The central IT should just monitor and advise, in case there are unwanted side effects. Any attempt towards strict regulation and formal approval processes will kill the benefits. In addition, younger employees who have grown up with computing power right from their infancy won't be happy about not being able to arrange their business tools according their immediate needs.

6.6 Summary

When we take the concepts of SOA and use them to shape business interactions between people, teams and units, a very new type of organization emerges: flexible, self-optimizing and potentially very open for interactions across organizational boundaries. It shows how services, combined with some technology that people use to communicate, can spark off a radical new way of doing business.

For larger organizations, this new model also needs some guidance and structure, whether they be repositories or organizational items (new roles and task definitions, decision and authority units, a basic law or rules of business conduct etc.).

While your business might not be ready for such a change, it will be valuable to assess whether or not newcomers could easily enter the market using such a model. And if they did, what would it mean for your position in this market?

However, the organization alone does not guarantee success. There also have to be people with suitable roles and attitudes to live the service oriented enterprise, as will be discussed in Chapter 7.

7 Service oriented people

7.1 Introduction

As shown in our SO Organization chapter and previously in the fundamental thoughts about business transformation, there are certain organizational and operational elements that can be applied to achieve appropriate results. However, the people have always been and always will be the key factor for the operation of the enterprise. They will also be the most important asset to master the new challenges that every organization has to face. Adapting a Service Oriented Architecture requires service oriented people.

This chapter discusses two important aspects of service oriented people: the roles people take on in a service oriented enterprise and the implications for individuals, their skills, their personal profiles, and their behaviour. Both will prove to be essential to the success of the enterprise.

The changes in the global economy require the highest agility from competing enterprises. This is why a greater-than-ever degree of flexibility and orientation toward customers and market demands is required from individuals in the enterprise.

7.2 Roles for SOA

The roles described in this chapter are abstracted from real-life organizations. Whether there is a single person for any of the roles, or one person assuming more than one role, or a group of people jointly playing a specific role, depends on the specific situation of an enterprise. When talking about roles, we intend to highlight specific tasks and responsibilities embedded in the service oriented organization of the company.

As Peter Weill and Jeanne W. Ross [Weill 2004] demonstrate in their work about IT Governance, there is not just one organizational form to achieve best-performing enterprises. On the contrary, there are certain combinations of decision rights and rules, institutions, teams, ways of installing deciders, and other criteria that determine the success of governing IT in the enterprise.

The demand for a closer link between business and IT was previously argued to be one of the core ingredients of successful implementation of SOA, or, as postulated in several analysts' statements, there is the identified need for IT to align with any line of business in the enterprise. This means IT is no longer seen as a mere task-executing operation unit that just costs, but its value contribution to the business in general, as well in concrete business cases, is now recognized.

With more services available, and more 'SOA infrastructure' to quickly realize new IT solutions, IT will become less technical in nature, and gain more business knowledge. IT will become a true partner of the business. No longer do the business units just throw requirements over the fence for IT departments to solve, deliver, and maintain for the benefit of business operations, there will be a genuine dialogue. If, in the past, the ultimate solution often did not really match the business needs, or it took too long for IT to deliver the right solution, business units very often went independently to the market for the best-fitting solutions, which they subsequently acquired and gave to the IT departments to integrate and maintain, without involving the latter in the purchase decision.

The result can be seen in nearly any enterprise today, where still over 80% of all effort is required to integrate and maintain myriads of point solutions, each of which has been built to cover not just a subject area, but all the surroundings too, in order to become a single solution of its own. Certainly software vendors and solution integrators did not have reuse and integration in a larger context in mind when building their solutions, as is now common within SOA. There is a lot of legacy – even just a couple of years old – that requires integration. Maintaining solutions that have been built for different platforms and environments also means that IT departments either have to maintain broad skill bases or get hooked up with vendors who can deliver such skills.

In the new situation where IT is getting closer to the business, we see the role of the enterprise architect as key.

7.2.1 The importance of the enterprise architect as the mediator between business and IT

The skills profile for a person in the role of mediating enterprise architect is certainly wider than that of, let's say, a software developer or a business process owner in any given business unit. However, at the same time, the knowledge and experience does not reach as deep as it does with those experts.

Figure 7.1 depicts several key areas of expertise and the added value of the enterprise architect in an organization. His or her role is to balance the objectives of both sides. The primary business needs are to act as flexibly as possible on the market, to increase revenue, and to comply with the growing set of rules and regulations imposed by political and industrial institutions. Similarly, IT has to follow certain standards, either those voluntarily set by themselves as enterprise-wide rules, or those developed by the IT industry, independent groups (open source), or vendors respectively. In parallel, IT has to deliver on the requirements that prescribe the desired solutions for the consumers in the company.

Due to the special situation of a SOA-based infrastructure, IT will act as the provider of measurements to the business (monitoring so-called 'key performance indicators') but also to themselves (e.g., performance data for which service level agreements have been made).

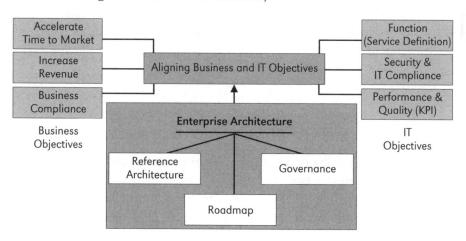

Figure 7.1 Enterprise architect as mediator between business and IT

An enterprise architect in a service oriented enterprise must be aware of this context and understand the concerns of both the business and IT to a sufficient degree so that he is able to mediate between the often-contradictory priorities from each side. Specific tasks and responsibilities are covered by means of creating reference architecture, the roadmap towards SOA for the specific company at hand and its business units, and finally caring for governance as described in one of the previous chapters.

Whether the enterprise architect has his or her background in IT, the COO organization, or a specific business unit, is not of primary concern. More important is the acceptance of the role of the individual (or, in cases of a larger enterprise, the team of enterprise architects) by both sides. Generally, this acceptance cannot be realized by decree but has to be earned through demonstrated skills and talent. Capacities like diplomacy and leadership are especially required.

An example of a typical task for an enterprise architect is to compose the SOA roadmap for the company, for example based on the maturity model that will be described in Chapter 8. The enterprise architect's role is to lead the definition of the enterprise's specific roadmap and coordinate the work needed for success. This requires interaction and diplomatic skills to mediate often contradictory or divergent interests between business and IT.

As described, the role of the enterprise architect takes a central position between the two camps of IT specialists and the business. This role generally heads the SOA Center of Excellence or other governance institutions responsible for the journey towards SOA in the enterprise. But it also involves a larger number of specialist roles that are described in the following sections.

7.2.2 Other key roles under SOA

Among the other key roles that play in an enterprise, we describe those that are most often met in practice. As mentioned previously, a role can be executed by one or more people. Also it is possible that a single person perform different roles in an enterprise. This depends mainly on the size of the organization.

The Business Service Champion
The Business Service Champion is the linchpin in the transformation to Service Oriented Architecture, bringing deep understanding of business and IT to

the programme. The role must be filled by an individual who is highly respected by both the business and IT organizations. The BSC will hold a position on the SOA CoE (Center of Excellence) Board that is normally introduced as one of the elements for organizing SOA Governance. Besides the identified IT seniors (the enterprise architect, BSC, and other senior professionals, depending on the size of the enterprise) each major line of business should be 'virtually' represented on this board by trusted delegates.

As stated, a BSC role for the enterprise architect role likewise requires deep understanding of both business process and IT capabilities. The focus, however, is on business process issues to drive the planning of services and solutions. A person in this role has the credibility to identify business process problems and lead the planning for IT and business changes in a given area.

Additionally, an extremely good understanding of SOA and Business Modeling concepts is expected, and the person in this role must understand the enterprise governance model and compliance measurements. Managing SOA-CoE relationships and expectations belongs to the tasks whose aim is to produce a successful estimate of the service scope and efforts. Finally, the use of industrial best practices knowledge adds to the skill pattern of a business service champion.

In this role, solutions are developed and must be sold to business and IT equally. As with all people on the CoE board, it is certainly not an easy task to balance short-term business improvements with longer-term strategic transformation in this context. This can be achieved when tying together visions on business and on IT architecture, coming back to the fundamentally close link between IT and business, which was postulated earlier and which incorporates the base for any SOA.

The Service Registrar

The Service Registrar is the gatekeeper of the organization's service metadata, leveraging existing reuse repositories. The Service Registrar augments asset repositories with service-appropriate metadata and search capabilities. He or she also helps create and assist in the enforcement of the organizational discipline necessary for populating the repository. The Service Registrar prevents the creation of redundant services by making it easy for project teams to scan the repository before beginning design/development efforts on a new service.

A person fulfilling the role of a Service Registrar needs to have very good understanding of SOA concepts, including bygone SOA technologies, should be skilled in developing service asset operating procedures with a SOA focus, and must have an expert understanding of metadata and search concepts and architectures. Further, in order to fulfil this role wholly, the individual or the group acting as service registrars should be experienced in implementing repository control processes with a focus on reusable components and services.

A person in the role of the service registrar has to implement and maintain the service repository tools and access interfaces, as well assist all involved parties with the service identification process. Building consensus around service publication in order to establish corporate policies and standards is also a responsibility, just like the enforcement of the policies and standards involved in service publication into the repository.

In this role, the service registrar supports the other CoE members and helps foster communication between service producers and consumers. In connection with the previously mentioned incentives or other governance means, this person can be obliged to monitor service use and reuse.

These three roles (the enterprise architect, the business service champion, and the service registrar), whether they be represented by three individuals, a larger team, or a single person in the enterprise, are the core of any successful transition into a service oriented enterprise.

In the following section we add a few more roles, or more accurately, aspects of work items encountered when setting up and operating a SOA-based IT shop. All of these roles have to co-operate very closely, utilizing the latest collaborative tools and means, including the service repository.

The Business Analyst
The Business Analyst harvests the functional requirements of business users, and provides domain knowledge to the team. They must understand the business language, and have industry and domain-specific skills. In a SOA approach, the Business Analyst should use methodologies like the ones presented in the chapter entitled 'Rethink your business'.

The Service Developer
The developer creates and tests the software implementation. In SOA, the role is not significantly different, with the exception of the code written in SOA projects, which is written as services – this turns the developer into a Service Developer.

The Security Specialist
The Security Specialist is responsible for the definition of security guidelines (policies) and the implementation of security means relevant to these guidelines. The guidelines are compliant with industry standards, as they also reflect the accepted policy of the individual enterprise in relation to business partners, e.g., acting in a supply chain as suppliers or development partners in the pharmaceutical industry.

The System and Database Administrator
This function performs the installation and provides ongoing maintenance on the technical infrastructure: the hardware, operating and database systems, and middleware. Certain aspects of information integration under SOA augment this typical role of the classic Database Administrator. It is essential to have skills that allow the development, management and maintenance of information services, as described in the context of the SOA reference architecture.

The Service Deployer
The Service Deployer takes the development artefacts and installs them in the target runtime environment.

The Service Integration Tester
The service integration tester is responsible for the various standard test stages, such as integration, load, and acceptance tests. He also defines test cases for service interoperability and conformance tests. This role is aligned to that of the architect and to the governance bodies, as described earlier. It is the quality assurance role.

The Tool Smith
The tool smith is responsible for designing and implementing the project-specific scripts, generators, and other utilities needed by various aspects of the SOA.

This role may decrease in importance as increasingly sophisticated development tools appear on the market. It always pays, however, to have a person who knows how to modify and adjust tools to the individual needs of the users, developers, and consumers in the enterprise. This person can even grow into an advisor, especially under the auspices of Web 2.0, where business users generally come to modify their workplace as needed for their individual daily work.

The Knowledge Transfer Facilitator

This role provides access to subject-matter experts and technical instructors who bring in extended knowledge regarding SOA, and, in most cases, Web services concepts and implementation assets. By relating the use cases created during the requirements gathering to the functions of this role, this role can easily be taken by so-called 'customer proxies' that represent individual service requests within the SOA. A particular feature of this role is the support given to the registrar; this role may be part of the registrar's job, depending on the size of the teams.

The SOA Project Manager

This role is an evolution of the classic project manager. The SOA project manager not only needs to plan for much shorter delivery cycles, but he or she must also establish new acceptance models. The project manager has to work with service providers to establish the appropriate service level agreements and resource usage. This role becomes more important with an increased use of aggregated services (those that are composed of other services).

The SOA System Administrator

In this role, in addition to managing and monitoring the platform infrastructure, the system administrator also manages the business and service level agreements within the SOA. In many cases, this role supports the above-described key role of the service registrar, but the SOA systems administrator is an administrative position rather than a proactive one.

The Process Flow Designer

Instead of an integration specialist, this role investigates the explicit, declarative possibilities of service orchestration (aggregation, composition). It concentrates on the technical process flows that support given business processes. This role is gaining in importance due to the accepted standard of BPEL and an increasing number of business-process modeling tool providers that enable a bridge between business process design and executable processes.

As there are more basic services available that can be combined into business relevant component services, the automation of the process flow increases and, correspondingly, the responsibility of this role also intensifies. SOA allows a more rapid implementation of changing business processes that match changing situations.

The Interoperability Tester

The interoperability tester verifies that any developed requestor and provider implementations will interoperate seamlessly. Another primary activity is to ensure Web Services Interoperability (WSI) conformance and industry standard conformance.

The Registry Administrator

The registry administrator defines how a generic registry data model can be customized and populated with services. In most cases, this is an optional role. It also depends on whether a standard is chosen, or if there is an alternative proprietary data model in the organization. In this case, there might be another similar role, often part of the IT Governance body, which acts as the SOA system administrator or which can be found in the role of the service registrar.

7.3 The impact on individuals

It is not just the skills that change or get redefined when dealing with SOA, but there are certain impacts on the personal attitudes, talents, and behaviours within a service oriented organization that are also important. Understanding services and service components as the core elements of a SOA, the people in the enterprise themselves become service consumers and service providers, as discussed under the SO organization topic.

In order to profit to the maximum from the loosely coupled service pattern of SOA, each professional is assigned more decision rights and power at hand so that he or she can perform without detailed management approvals or detailed instructions; one simply adheres to the general set of rules and regulations. This means the enterprise as a whole becomes more agile and can react to customer demands much quicker.

7.3.1 The SO professional

For the individual in the organization this also means more responsibility, more exposure, and less excuses of the art: 'I was told to do this way', or 'the rules in this case said that ...'. As industrial production has gradually become increasingly automated, we now face a period of business-process automation, where all standard business routines are being programmed for execution by IT. Human interaction has become similarly peripheral to the manufacturing industry; nowadays it provides input and takes the final results, as well as monitoring the processes.

The advanced technologies that help build choreographed execution of services or business components nowadays allow a rather flexible definition of business processes. Does this mean that the individual has to become a programmed unit? Certainly not! The long-term trend in manufacturing shows that humans fulfil an initiating, monitoring and controlling role in both simple and relatively complex activities, but repetitive working operations have been taken over by machines.

Analogous to plant operation, administrative work and a growing number of services have been automated in order to support the various business units: the sales force with on-the-spot information about the customers and their economic situation, tax accountants with intelligently formulated rules (which always change rapidly), tellers with suitable offerings to the individual customer in front of them, and many more.

Often, automated steps have to change suddenly, but still show a familiar interface to the system users. The previously described core feature of SOA, namely separation of concerns as shown in the SOA reference architecture, allows the exchange of certain business application services (e.g., a new formula to calculate interest rates or tax dues) or even a completely rearranged business process without changes in the user interface or in the database structure or any integrated legacy applications, if there is no real need.

In time, employees will learn how to draw information, how to use information services for their immediate needs in an *ad hoc* manner. Filling in an organizational structure like the human services bus will require more of this type of active behaviour from the people involved. On the other hand, common experience with the internet has prepared almost everyone for such activities, as people are accustomed to searching for all kinds of information or goods and contacts online. Even more future generations will take it as something natural, without reservations.

Aspects of privacy, access control, and related political topics will certainly be newly discussed in the light of global markets and worldwide labour forces. Just recently, workers' unions started to rethink their positions and get together in global organizations, as an increasing number of enterprises extend their activities globally, either as a single unit or in business partnerships around the globe.

7.3.2 The SO manager role

The roles and responsibilities of managers in a service oriented enterprise are going to change towards a strongly monitoring approach to the running system, in accordance with their set rules in the organization structure. In order to gain the maximum from the assigned teams and business units, the managers will be asked to 'empower' their employees and provide the appropriate tools, access rights, and rules that allow them to react to their customers as quickly, adequately, and as needed in any given situation.

A part of this is to plan, deploy, and measure new business processes and utilize the power of SOA in this sense to make the company as agile as required. As human interaction within a human services bus, or simply in any given process, has been designed to work according to roles, required skills and talents, the responsibility for managers is to staff adequately.

In many cases, employee skills are collected and maintained on the basis of certification, graduation, and classes attended. This provides quite a good view on the cognitive capabilities of the individual. But in order to get the best results in a service oriented economy, there are other non-technical aspects that need to be dealt with.

As shown in several experiments and in real-life experiences, there are sociological and psychological traits and aspects that determine the success of a group, and finally of an enterprise. These research results indicate that successfully operating teams and companies do not merely display optimized structures and efficient operation, they also possess certain human components that turn the balance. Generally spoken, the best results from any team will be obtained when a specific mix of employees' talents, skills, and temperaments can be realized. As a manager, one has to ensure that one gets exactly this mix on board.

There are tools to support this managerial task, e.g., employee registries that allow the presentation of not only technical knowledge or achieved educational grades, but also capture the talents and temperament of the individual, showing exactly which tasks, duties, activities one likes or dislikes doing. An employees' registry showing individual talents and preferences is ideal for enabling people managers to staff as required. It indicates features such as who can best co-operate with others, thus helping to avoid friction among co-workers.

Certain sociological and psychological skills are required from a manager under these conditions. But there are motivators who know to find the 'sweet spot' in any person in order to achieve a common goal, delivering a demanded service to the customer at that level of satisfaction that makes the client return and happily pay for it.

Scientific research results show that in any society, organization or group that is large enough, one can find a sufficient number of the required individual traits that are needed for any given project. If dealing with smaller organizational units, it is necessary to form co-operative links beyond the limits. To realize these, there are upcoming platforms, tools, and advice available to enable goal-oriented, i.e., service oriented operation on any given occasion.

As a reader, you may not be immediately convinced, but we ask you to consider your personal situation – whether it be as a manager or in some other professional role. Think of your individual contribution to meeting the company goals, to realizing the corporate strategy of the unit you work for. Here you will quickly find that in order to reach monetary goals – add to the bottom line – one needs to deal with lots of unpredictable situations, often caused by humans. If you succeed in identifying any single step you take as part of the corporate journey, if you can find your personal talents being used to achieve the goals, your personal motivation will be stimulated and effort will be undertaken, often beyond business-as-usual levels.

In the chapter on organization, we spoke about service level agreements (SLA) between the various service providers and service consumers. These levels are individually influenced by the motivation of the employees involved. If you can manage to raise this, the SLAs can be adjusted and a more satisfied

8 How to prepare for SOA

8.1 Introduction

The principles of SOA are quite simple and easy to understand, its value has been made evident, but now, where to start? Back in the natural environment, about to begin the journey, the landscape looks more like a path winding deep into the jungle rather than a straight, wide, and well-signposted route. The big picture is quite clear, but defining a strategy, a roadmap, is tricky and disorienting.

A global approach – enterprise-wide and often top-down – is hazardous at the very least. It implies filling a huge organizational and technological gap, which most of the board members will, rightfully, hesitate to do. Failures of past grandiose and promising IT initiatives have diminished their enthusiasm for very large investments.

On the other hand, confining SOA to a too-small scope and potential gain, taking no risk, will cement the initiative at the status of an anecdotic episode, with no real interest for the organization.

Deploying an as-is integrated SOA solution, hoping that it will deliver all the expected benefits, can also be tempting. That kind of project can certainly work, since the technology has become more mature and an increasing number of SOA skills are to be found. Nevertheless, it doesn't fit the whole scope, as it focuses only on pragmatic IT issues.

As always, the solution has to be tailored to one's context, needs, and goals. The stronger and weaker points of the organization must be taken into account in a progressive approach. This chapter describes the characteristics and some of the unavoidable steps to be followed when using such an approach. But first of all, a clear view of the situation is necessary to define and prioritize the first steps. This chapter provides a tool to help assess the SOA maturity of your organization so that you can prepare for SOA. The maturity model shows whether you are ready for only some SOA projects or for an enterprise-wide deployment of SOA. It also tells you which areas to improve when you decide to deploy SOA on an enterprise-wide scale.

8.2 SOA Maturity Model

Why a Maturity Model?

SOA involves many different disciplines and crafts because it is at the interface of architecture, IT, and business. New processes are needed, which implies adapting the organization. An implementation of SOA will continuously evolve, will need to be aligned, managed and, let's say the word: governed. It is not a target which can be reached once and for all, since the goal of SOA is to support the business goals and to adapt to the new challenges that companies face. So, successfully improving the SOA abilities of an organization can only be achieved by handling several simultaneous threads upfront, but at different speeds and according to the current maturity level of each of the carefully identified key areas.

The maturity model presented below reflects the multi-dimensional characteristic of SOA.

Description of the SOA Maturity Model

The model is based on a maturity matrix composed of key areas: subjects that must be addressed and maturity levels that can be reached for each of the levels. This matrix is supported by checkpoints enabling the measurement of the maturity level.

Key areas

The model identifies 20 different areas which need specific attention in order to achieve a comprehensive SOA. These key areas are grouped into the following categories: Process, Technology, and People.

- Process deals with areas that are very closely related to embedding architecture and governance in an organization, the two main prerequisites for SOA.
- Technology is the second category which focuses on the way systems are decomposed and made flexible and the standards that are used.
- People deals with skills, mindset, and the necessary knowledge when implementing SOA.

Categories	No.	Key area
Process	1	Commitment and motivation
	2	Relationships with projects
	3	Roles and responsibility
	4	Development of architecture
	5	Use of architecture
	6	Architectural tools (methodology and software)
	7	Quality Management
	8	Service portfolio management
	9	Vision of architecture
	10	Alignment Information Systems with business
	11	Budgeting and planning
Technology	12	Technology and standards
	13	Componentization and Reuse
	14	Business processes implementation in Information systems
	15	Information systems (infrastructure and applications) flexibility
	16	Security
People	17	SOA skills IT
	18	SOA skills Business
	19	SOA mindset and knowledge among IT People
	20	SOA mindset and knowledge among Business People

Table 8.1 Twenty key areas of SOA maturity

Maturity levels

In order to have insight into the state of the key areas, the model supplies them with a range of levels, from A (lowest) to D (highest). On average, there are three levels for each key area. Each higher level is better than its preceding level in terms of time (faster), money (cheaper), and/or quality (better). By using levels, we can unambiguously assess the current situation of SOA in the organization. It also increases the ability to advise on targets for gradual improvement. Each level consists of certain requirements for the key area. The requirements, or checkpoints, of a certain level also comprise the requirements of lower levels: a key area at level B fulfils the requirements of both level A and B. If the requirements for level A are not satisfied, it is considered to be at the lowest and, consequently, undefined level for that particular key area.

Maturity level checkpoints

In order to determine levels, the SOA Maturity Model is supported by an objective measuring instrument. The requirements for each level are defined in the form of checkpoints: questions that need to be answered positively in order to qualify for that level. Based on the checkpoints, the SOA maturity can be assessed, and the proper level can be established for each key area. As each next level of a key area is considered an improvement, this means that the checkpoints are cumulative: in order to classify for level B, the key area needs to answer positively to the checkpoints of both level B and level A.

8.3 Twenty key areas of SOA maturity

We have broken down a SOA practice into 20 areas that must be represented in performing a SOA practice. These areas will be explained briefly per category.

1. Commitment and motivation

The commitment and motivation of SOA stakeholders are important drivers for the success of creating and using SOA in an organization. There are many stakeholders of SOA: business and IT managers, architects, process and product developers, engineers, testers, and project and program managers, who must first accept, then understand and commit to the choice of SOA, thus acknowledging its strategic value. Starting as an isolated choice, SOA then becomes fully integrated in all organizational processes.

2. Relationships with projects

SOA is implemented through projects. Therefore projects need to start complying with SOA-based architectures, standards, and guidelines. Projects can then become an important source for technical and non-technical feedback and ideas. Accordingly, a constructive dialogue between architects and project teams will be built for the benefit of both: architects will learn from the practical experience in projects and the project managers will understand why they have to comply with constraints. This relationship aligns projects and architecture, and takes each stakeholder's constraints into account.

3. Roles and responsibilities

Explaining the roles and responsibilities of architects will prevent and solve many disagreements and differences of understanding. It clarifies who can be held accountable for their contribution to the architecture. When starting a SOA, the IT department will probably be in charge of the architecture and process. In more mature organizations, the responsibility of process owner-ship is transversal.

If roles and responsibilities are unclear, there is a chance that the implemen-tation will fail, ending up in an organizational vacuum.

4. Architecture development

Developing SOA-based architecture can be done in different ways, varying from isolated, autonomous projects to a continuous facilitating process. The more the architecture development process is embedded in an organization as a continuous process, the more a SOA-based architecture will be experi-enced as added value.

5. Use of architecture

Developing SOA-based architecture is not a goal in itself. Architecture ought to be used in an organization to achieve the goals for which it has been devel-oped. Architecture can be used in various ways: purely informative, to guide individual projects, or as a management instrument for the complete organi-zation.

6. Architectural tools (methodology and software)

Developing SOA-based architecture demands methodologies consisting of activities, techniques, tools, and products. When tools are fully integrated in the process of developing architecture, preferably supported by a repository, their effectiveness and efficiency is greatest. In case of SOA, the full integra-tion of business, information, and technical modeling is ultimately recom-mended.

7. Quality management

The quality of SOA-based architecture is important for its successful imple-mentation. Quality management is meant to assure that quality, or at least the value produced by implemented architectures, will be measured through ret-roactive assessment, which can be informal or indicator-based. A quality process can be progressively created and integrated into the organization's level of quality process.

8. Service portfolio management

SOA is, of course, service-based. Services are identified, designed, built, changed and, at some point, decommissioned. The scope and life cycle of services have to be managed from a service portfolio approach in accordance with the goals and policies of the organization. The basic approach is to couple service and application management. But the development of cross-application reused services benefit induces the need for distinct life cycles and, ultimately, funding.

9. Vision of IS architecture

Information Systems (IS) need flexibility to adapt and evolve in line with business goals. Flexibility doesn't mean improvising *ad hoc* changes at the last minute but requires proactive action. In order to respond proactively to the necessary changes, a clear vision is needed of not only the current state of information systems, but also of the necessary short and long-term evolutions in order to face the technological and, most importantly, business challenges and goals.

10. Alignment with business

SOA-based architecture finds its justification in enabling the realization of business goals. Meeting them is a start, but supporting the planned business changes and facilitating the business transformation are the ultimate goals. Therefore, in adapting architecture to business demands, the degree to which the architecture process is tuned to the business goals and capabilities is crucial.

11. Budgeting and planning

The implementation of SOA needs budgeting and planning. To prevent SOA initiatives from drifting and to make them more tangible, it is necessary to plan and budget SOA projects. This may vary from calculating the ROI of every single project to continuously optimizing the planning-and-control process.

12. Technology and standards

SOA has to be implemented on a solid technological ground in order to deliver the intended benefits. The technology and standards have to be chosen carefully. This process of choosing can vary from *ad hoc* adoption to the anticipation of new standards and technologies.

13. Componentization and reuse

Adaptability is achieved through reuse. Reuse needs componentization. This reuse by componentization is not a spontaneous evolution. Some results can be achieved by capitalizing from one project to another but the real value is

delivered by deliberately designing, planning, managing, and, the most difficult but most efficient of all, funding.

14. Business processes implementation in the Information System

SOA implies that business processes are implemented as part of an information system. This can be done within the existing silos to begin with, and then
extended to end-to-end monitored processes across business lines that lead
to a continuous improvement of the organization's efficiency.

15. Information System flexibility (infrastructure and applications)

Organizations are traditionally organized within silos running their own
applications, hardware, and functionalities. These information system structures will be split up and recomposed into modular, flexible, reuseable and
shareable components. Information systems will be virtualized; it is no longer
relevant which platform a component runs on.

16. Information security

The security of distributed systems and components in a SOA environment
is a commonly recognized concern. Web services security will (soon) be
addressed by standards and products. Other issues, such as organization security policy, legal responsibility between business partners, and secure communication over shared infrastructure, demand attention and agreement.
Information security can vary from a reactive attitude to a largely proactive
attitude based on an information security policy.

17. SOA skills in IT

In a SOA environment, the IT professionals involved must have the proper
skills. IT professionals on whom SOA has a high impact include: IT architects,
information analysts, designers, software engineers, infrastructure engineers,
testers, and maintenance engineers.

18. SOA skills in Business

In a SOA environment, the business professionals involved must have the
proper skills. Business professionals on whom SOA has a high impact include:
enterprise and business architects, business analysts, process designers, testers, and functional maintenance employees.

19. SOA mindset and knowledge among IT people

Service orientation is not only an architectural style but also a way of thinking
in terms of services and reusing these services, instead of reinventing the

wheel. IT people must understand and use this paradigm so that the organization becomes eager to reap the benefits of SOA. One of the challenges for IT people is to think in terms of reuse rather than in terms of re-building what already exists.

20. SOA mindset and knowledge among Business people

Service orientation is not only an architectural style but also a way of thinking in terms of services and re-using these services. Business people must understand and use this paradigm so that the organization becomes eager to reap the benefits of SOA. One of the challenges for business people is to think in reusable functionalities and to decouple a business process from the functionalities (services) that will be used in such a process.

8.4 Not everything needs to happen at once

Each of the 20 factors in effective SOA practices must receive sufficient attention. This does not mean, however, that each must be given equal consideration at all times.

First of all, not every factor is equally relevant at the start. Quality Management will certainly become a key concern at some point, but organizations that are still in the phase of building up a SOA practice can focus more productively on commitment and motivation, vision of architecture, technology and standards, information security, and SOA mindset and knowledge. Quality Management will have its turn.

Furthermore, any given area need not be brought up to its full state of development right away. Different levels of maturity can be distinguished in each of the various areas. Commitment and motivation undergo several growth stages. SOA is often initially approached by funding a couple of SOA initiatives. At a higher level of maturity, the SOA approach is sponsored by the management of the organization: SOA is considered to be of importance for the organization. In the final stage, SOA is ultimately viewed as a process that is integrated with other organization processes.

As a result of this differentiated growth, each key area has its own path of development, distinguishable into meaningful levels. The nature and the number of levels in each path depend entirely on the character of the individual concern and are established independently of all the other concerns.

As shown in Table 8.2, in actual practice the path of development in most areas passes through three or four levels.

Distinguishing key areas, each having its own developmental path, makes it possible to implement and optimize SOA practices step by step. It provides guidance in giving the proper amount of attention to each area of concern at the proper time. Using it, the organization can take manageable measures for improvement in those areas offering the greatest added value in the light of the as-is state of the organization. To do this, we must determine the optimal course the organization should take to navigate through all the cells in the next table. Which level should we endeavour to attain in a particular area at any given time? The answer to this question is compiled in a SOA Maturity Model.

	Key area	**Level A**	**Level B**	**Level C**	**Level D**
1	Commitment and motivation	Budget and time available for SOA initiatives	SOA approach is sponsored by the management of the organization	SOA approach is integrated in the organization process	
2	Relationships with projects	Architecture to project communication	Architectural process takes projects feedback into account	Architects, business and IT jointly build the project architecture	Continuous dialogue between architects, business and IT
3	Roles and responsibility	IT department in charge of architecture and process	IT and business collaborate in architectural process	Responsibility of process ownership is transversal	
4	Development of architecture	Architecture undertaken in projects	Architecture as a transversal process	Architecture as a facilitation process	
5	Use of architecture	Architecture used informatively	Architecture used to steer content	Architecture integrated into the organization	

	Key area	Level A	Level B	Level C	Level D
6	Architectural tools (methodology and software)	Non-coordinated initiatives	Tooling streamlining and integration policy, global architecture process defined	Tooling is comprehensive and integrated, global architecture process formalized	
7	Quality Management	Afterwards, non-formal validation	A retroactive assessment is done on the basis of standardized indicators	The IS architecture quality process is defined. Continuous quality management	The IS architecture quality process is integrated in the organization quality process
8	Service portfolio management	Life cycles of services follow those of applications delivering them	Service level agreements	Planned life cycle (including decommissioning)	Service usage funding (service market place)
9	Vision of architecture	Vision of 'as-is' architecture	Vision of short-term evolutions	Vision of long-term architecture	Continuous alignment of vision with business goals, short and long-term
10	Alignment Information Systems with business	Applications and services are designed to meet business goals (business driven)	Applications and services are tested for compatibility with business goals	Architectural process supports the business	Architectural process facilitates business transformation
11	Budgeting and planning	Need to formally justify a direct ROI for each impacted SOA business project	SOA project specific	Organization generic	Continuous optimization of the budgeting and planning process

	Key area	Level A	Level B	Level C	Level D
12	Technology and standards	Ad hoc technology chosen when needed	IT base referential defined and proven	Motivated strategy	Anticipation of technological changes and new standards adoption
13	Componentization and Reuse	Non-coordinated reuse	Reuse is coordinated within IT (technical services)	Reuse is coordinated on the business level (business services)	Business and IT are componentized and reuse is a common practice
14	Business processes implementation in Information systems	Existing business services within silos	Transversal process	Business Activity Monitoring (BAM)	Business and IT collaborates to build and deploy business processes
15	Information systems (infrastructure and applications) flexibility	Silo-based information systems containing service-based application and hardware running them	Some applications and infrastructure are shared among (hazy) silos due to rationalization	Urbanized, reconfigurable and process-oriented information system	Decoupled business – information systems virtualization
16	Security	Reactive	Individual	Collective	Proactive
17	SOA skills in IT	Basic	Moderate	Experienced	
18	SOA skills in Business	Basic	Moderate	Experienced	
19	SOA mindset and knowledge among IT People	Sparse awareness	Organization level awareness	Common SOA mindset	
20	SOA mindset and knowledge among Business People	Sparse awareness	Organization level awareness	Common SOA mindset	

Table 8.2 Maturity levels per key area

149

The Chaos Case

Don't worry, you won't start SOA from scratch. If you have that impression, just try to imagine what the practices would look like in an organization that scores zero on all of the key areas in the maturity model. The imaginary case below is based on a mix of several real-life cases.

Commitment and Motivation

The business managers have heard about SOA, and, to them, it is obviously the latest technical hype. IT will deal with it on their budget since an IT manager is responsible for the SOA initiative. The problem is that this guy is much too busy maintaining the current system.

Budgeting and Planning

Maintenance devours 75% of the money allocated to IT. So maybe, says the IT guy, if a big, new, high-priority project with special funding starts up, he could start a SOA study in parallel, and finance it by raising the bill on this high-priority project by a modest 10%.

Alignment of Information Systems with Business

So, for now, let's keep a low profile. Relationships between Business & IT are tense enough as they are ... Well, officially everything is fine: the number of requests from the business lines that are refused by IT is very low. But the truth is that business avoids asking IT to do anything since implementing any solution always takes too long (at least 6 months) and is much too expensive (a 6-digit figure).

Business Processes Implementation in the Information System

Leaving the IT manager, you remember that you had heard about several reasons behind those problems. The core business applications runs on a mainframe, there are many newer applications on UNIX systems, some portals. Each application fulfils a specific function, manages its own data. Until recently, when needed, connections were created between all of them. But this has become a ball of spaghetti that no one now knows how to unravel.

Information System (infrastructure and applications) flexibility

Last year a 'consultation data warehouse' was implemented. Every night, new data from every application is stored in the data warehouse. The new applications use the warehouse as a data referential. For now, it makes it possible to plug new applications in without having to manage the connections.

Information Security
But since the warehouse does not work in real time, some applications use data which has already been modified by another application. There are many instances of data incoherence between applications. IT is working hard detecting and correcting the mistakes.

Relationships with Projects
Another angle of approach, you think, could be to find a starting project which could comply with a basic SOA, designed by the architects of the organization. Unfortunately, as some IT operations managers will tell you, projects often refuse to use the architectural standards and design unique, *ad hoc* architectures. They claim that the instructions 'dropped down from the Ivory Tower' cannot be implemented, they just don't work.

Roles and Responsibility
So, maybe refactoring the architecture referential and redefining target architecture could help starting a virtuous circle. After spending some time sending a few emails, making phone calls, and drinking coffee with some of your colleagues, you reach the conclusion that architects wear several hats and the architecture is modified by whoever is available when something really has to be done.

Development of Architecture
Consequently, architecture is developed within projects, if someone thinks about doing it at all.

Use of Architecture
And anyway, the proposed architecture often remains unused for the reasons mentioned above.

Vision of Architecture
As a result, architectural description is scattered throughout the project's documentation, if not only stored in the minds of the project teams.

Architectural Tools (Methodology and Software)
If you could gather all the documentation which has been produced, you would find a heterogeneous collection of UML: meridian diagrams made with different software (with or without a proper licence), textual description, PowerPoint presentations, etc. which are, most of the time, out of date.

Quality Management
The results of the architecture can, of course, never be assessed since the project architects are assigned from one project to another.

SOA Skills
Actually, the project architects are often young and motivated software designers who do their best to build decent architecture, like the one who told you about this book. Last time you saw him, he told you he was leaving the company.

Componentization and Reuse
He worked in the 'web service competency center' of your organization. He participated in the development of an XML toolbox embedding the description of all the business objects, the common vocabulary of the company. Due to a shortage of resources, he tried to capitalize from one project to another; but the cost of adapting what had been previously done was prohibitive and most of the time projects were started from scratch all over again.

Service Portfolio Management
His team managed to have web services developed by projects but since nobody organized it, a web-service pandemic spread throughout the applications. At some point, the services had to be shut down one after the other: if a user complained, it meant that the service was still in use. Otherwise, it was disengaged.

SOA Mindset & Knowledge
Desperate, you put this book in a drawer and firmly decide to forget about SOA. However you will never forget the lesson that you have learned that successful implementation of SOA requires mature IT and business practices throughout the organization.

8.5 Using the SOA Maturity Model

Once the level of maturity for each key area has been measured, the results must be used to determine which actions for improvement are required. These actions must then be prioritized. Of course, not all of the key areas are equally important and achieving a certain level of maturity in one key area can depend on the realization of another. There is no point in managing the quality delivered by the architecture if the vision of this architecture is not clear. Many interdependencies can be found between the various levels of key areas.

Therefore, all levels and key areas are related to each other in a SOA Maturity Model in Table 8.3. This has been done to determine the internal priorities and interdependencies between levels and key areas. The vertical axis of the matrix indicates key areas and the horizontal axis shows scales of maturity. In the matrix, each level is related to a specific grade of the 13 scales of maturity. When a box remains empty, this is an indication that achieving a higher maturity for a key area does not depend on the maturity of another key area. Finally there is no gradation between the levels: as long as a key area is not entirely classified at level B, it remains at level A.

The purpose of this Model is to give all of the stakeholders a clear view of their SOA maturity. The strengths and weaknesses will appear graphically on a single easy-to-use chart. This assists the process of defining the points for improvement and discussing a strategy and action plan for moving to a level of greater efficiency.

The Model enables the identification of what already works well or just needs to be fine-tuned, what can be relied on, and what must be improved, implemented, or done in a different way.

The Model works from left to right, so that key areas whose levels have a low grade on the scale must be improved first. As a consequence of the interdependencies between levels and key areas, the areas on the right of the Model will offer less return on investment if they are implemented before the others.

In this way, it is possible to work one step at a time towards stage 13. However, this final stage represents a measure of perfection that not every organization wishes to attain. The principle of 'just enough, just in time' also applies to SOA practice. It is more sensible to set a lower stage as an initial target: stage 3, for example. Once this goal has been achieved, the organization is more ready to deploy SOA and can then decide if this is sufficient, or perhaps it may wish to adopt a higher stage – stage 6, for example – as a new goal. In this process, it is possible to distinguish different stages as in Table 8.4.

	Key area	Stage													
		0	1	2	3	4	5	6	7	8	9	10	11	12	13
1	Commitment and motivation		A				B				C				
2	Relationships with projects				A			B		C				D	
3	Roles and responsibility			A			B			C					
4	Development of architecture			A				B			C				
5	Use of architecture				A				B			C			
6	Architectural tools (methodology and software)					A				B			C		
7	Quality Management						A			B			C		D
8	Service portfolio management					A			B			C			D
9	Vision of architecture		A		B		C							D	
10	Alignment with business			A			B			C			D		
11	Budgeting and planning				A			B			C			D	
12	Technology and standards		A				B						C		D
13	Componentization and Reuse			A				B					C		D
14	Business processes implementation in the Information System				A					B			C		D
15	Information System (infrastructure and applications) flexibility			A		B							C		D
16	Information Security		A			B			C			D			
17	SOA skills in IT			A				B		C					
18	SOA skills in Business			A				B		C					
19	SOA mindset and knowledge among IT People		A				B			C					
20	SOA mindset and knowledge among Business People		A				B			C					

Table 8.3 SOA Maturity Model

Stage	SOA readiness	Characteristics
0	To execute a SOA pilot project	No awareness, no skills, no commitment, no standards, no guidelines, no best practices.
3	To execute SOA-related projects within isolated parts of the enterprise	The basics are in place, however a lot need to be learned and can be improved. It is important to have a process in which learning experiences can be incorporated and in which standards, guidelines and best practices will be developed and improved.
6	To execute SOA-related projects enterprise-wide	The number of standards, guidelines and best practices is growing. Experience is built up and reused in the enterprise.
9	To execute all SOA-related projects enterprise-wide as well as a SOA-related business transformation project	There is quite a lot of experience in deploying SOA. Standards, guidelines and best practices are broadly available and deployed enterprise-wide.
13	For a continuous business transformation	Deploying SOA is completely embedded in the processes of the enterprise. Products and processes are continuously optimized, triggered by internal and external drivers.

Table 8.4 Stages of SOA readiness

Our experience is that most organizations are still trying to attain stage 3 or have just reached that level. At that level, SOA has a reasonable profile. It produces some results, but things could be better. Organizations that have reached stage 6 will notice that they will have more success in employing SOA. From this stage, it may be worth considering whether or not it makes sense to continue to stage 9. Not every organization will choose to do so. Stage 9 will only yield additional returns if the organization is ready for it in other areas of structure and management.

There is, however, a preliminary step in setting goals and priorities: determining the current position of the organization with regard to the 20 key areas. The as-is state can be represented in the SOA Maturity Model in the manner illustrated in Table 8.5.

		Stage													
	Key area	0	1	2	3	4	5	6	7	8	9	10	11	12	13
1	Commitment and motivation		A				B				C				
2	Relationships with projects				A			B	C					D	
3	Roles and responsibility			A			B			C					
4	Development of architecture			A				B			C				
5	Use of architecture				A				B			C			
6	Architectural tools (methodology and software)					A				B			C		
7	Quality Management						A				B		C		D
8	Service portfolio management					A			B			C			D
9	Vision of architecture		A		B	C								D	
10	Alignment with business			A			B			C			D		
11	Budgeting and planning				A			B			C			D	
12	Technology and standards		A				B					C	D		
13	Componentization and Reuse			A				B					C		D
14	Business processes implementation in the Information System				A					B			C		D
15	Information System (infrastructure and applications) flexibility			A	B							C			D
16	Information Security		A			B			C			D			
17	SOA skills in IT			A				B			C				
18	SOA skills in Business			A				B			C				
19	SOA mindset and knowledge among IT People	A					B			C					
20	SOA mindset and knowledge among Business People	A					B			C					

Table 8.5 SOA Maturity Model for an example organization at stage 0

The organization in Table 8.5 is still at stage 0 because the area involving *SOA mindset and knowledge among Business People* has not been developed at all. The matrix shows that the organization should focus on this area. Once the basic A level is reached here, the organization will have attained stage 1. *SOA skills Business* is then the area that it subsequently has to work on, in order to advance to stage 3. In this fashion, we can concretely map out a path of development.

The SOA Maturity Model can be used for multiple goals:
- See what the sequence of developments will be with SOA.
  Read through the model and examine the sequence of developing aspects. Notice how the different aspects relate to one another.
- Gaining insight into the strengths and weaknesses of the current operation.
- Fill in the model describing the current situation. The aspects that score higher than average are your strengths, the aspects that score lower might need attention.
- Planning ahead.
  Determine the goals you want to achieve with SOA and make them explicit. Find the corresponding 'maturity level' in the model and fill in the model, describing the current situation. Make your roadmap by putting into sequence the aspects that need to be improved to reach the desired level.

8.6 Targeted action

Employing SOA involves many factors. We have defined 20 of them, each one with its own developmental path. That's too many to attend to all at once, so we use the SOA Maturity Model to bring things into focus. By representing the organization on this matrix, we can determine the key areas that must be emphasized in the near future and the extent to which this needs to be done. On this basis, we can plan targeted improvements.

For those who wish to make use of the SOA Maturity Model, Appendix 1 provides more detailed information. To establish where an organization stands, each area of concern has a number of checkpoints at every level. Using these checkpoints, it is possible to determine whether or not the organization has attained the appropriate level. If the organization does not fulfil all the checkpoints of a particular level, but nevertheless wishes to use the SOA Maturity Model to reach that level, the appropriate actions can be mapped out. These actions are, in part, derived from the checkpoints. At the same time, the actions must always suit the organization's circumstances. Formulating improvements should never be a purely mechanical process.

8.7 Summary

Starting any innovative initiative is never easy, especially if, as is the case with SOA, multiple domains of the organization are highly impacted. SOA has an avalanche of consequences. This is why, instead of a step-by-step methodology, we described the SOA Maturity Model that will point you in the right direction at the right pace towards a specific SOA target that best fits your organization. The SOA Maturity Model can be regarded as a compass and a machete to start cutting your way through the SOA jungle. It tells you exactly which areas to improve, depending on your level of ambition.

The SOA Maturity Model enumerates 20 factors impacting the successful implementation of SOA. And even this is a reduction, because many more factors have been discarded simply to keep the model usable. No organization has enough time, money and resources to deal with all those topics upfront, especially since SOA is certainly not a goal in itself but rather a means to facilitate business. That is why it is necessary to determine a strategy that addresses each issue at exactly the right time – not too early and definitely not too late.

Depending on each organization's industry sector, history and strategy, some key areas will have already been addressed to different extents. Furthermore, differences in business goals will make each organization's initial actions vary considerably.

Analysing the SOA Maturity Model can help in directing effort and investment to those areas that need it most. In this way, a medium-term, transversal strategy emerges, resulting in different projects to make your organization ready for SOA.

Besides these considerations, which strive to avoid wasting time and money on inefficient activities, a nascent SOA initiative must also build up credibility by rapidly delivering tangible results and value to the business. That is one of the most important reasons why SOA initiatives must always be tied into actual projects. In the next chapter we will discuss how to find suitable business projects.

9 How to start SOA

9.1 Introduction

You have decided to implement SOA. The previous chapter provided insight into the consequences and the impact this will entail. This chapter discusses how to draw up a roadmap for the implementation of SOA. Where to begin? Which steps do you need to take and when? Which preconditions have to be met? To what extent does a SOA project differ from any other project?

In this chapter, we first present an overall approach that indicates the steps that need to be taken to implement SOA. Then we deal more specifically with the so-called 'Entry Points' that describe characteristic SOA projects. Thinking in terms of Entry Points helps you to spot potential SOA projects in your organization and clarify the business value of these.

9.2 Your roadmap to SOA

Implementing SOA brings an avalanche of consequences. This also means that SOA can almost never be implemented in a single programme or project, but requires gradual implementation. This implementation is not driven by the objective of ultimately realizing SOA, but rather by the desire to realize the aims of the organization while making use of SOA as an architectural style.

The implementation of SOA is never a goal on its own. A first conclusion is that no SOA roadmap is needed – you require a roadmap that leads via SOA to the real objective, whatever that may be. This imposes the obligation to consider what SOA can mean to your organization and what the aims should be. In previous chapters, we advised you to conduct a strategic dialogue between business and IT and to formulate a business vision on SOA as a result. Only then will it become evident what SOA can signify to you and where the opportunities lie in its application. After all, SOA is not a revolution but an evolution, it is not a big bang. Once a policy has been drawn up to specify the way in which SOA can benefit an organization, subsequent concrete projects, initiated by the business, will implement this vision step by step. 'Think big, act small' is an approach that suits SOA very well.

Figure 9.1 provides an overview of SOA through time. The formulation of the SOA Roadmap is a component of this.

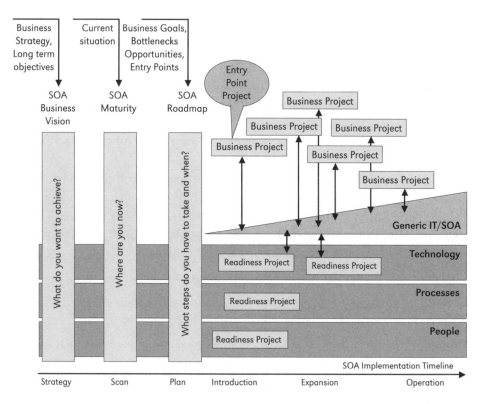

Figure 9.1 SOA Implementation Approach

The input for the SOA Roadmap consists of:
- The business vision on SOA. This is the strategic note in which the added value of SOA for your organization is recorded.
- The determination of position in the SOA Maturity Model. This indicates your strong and weak points in the Process, Technology and People areas.
- The concrete business aims, bottlenecks and opportunities for the actual deployment of SOA.
- The entry points that describe the characteristics of SOA projects.

The output is the SOA Roadmap with the following important components:
- Basic choices for layout and steering.
- Choice of business projects.
- Choice of readiness projects.

Making basic choices

The very first step in formulating a SOA Roadmap is to make a number of essential choices that are important in the implementation of SOA. The Table below lists these choices with a number of alternatives, along with their advantages and disadvantages. The choices mentioned here should be elaborated into principles that guide the SOA implementation. The principles must be embedded in the enterprise architecture of your organization.

Basic choice	Alternatives	Advantages	Disadvantages
Who formulates the service contract (specifications and conditions of a service)?	Project	Project gets the service it wants. Speed.	Little interest in reuse. Risk that various standards are applied.
	Central organ	Can transcend projects and has better view of reuse.	Risk that it will cause delay. Risk of ivory tower effect.
Who steers the service portfolio (and thus the service life cycle)?	Business	If the business is the owner of the services, it is logical that the service portfolio is also steered there.	Services are automated pieces of business functionality of which IT is often the only party that knows who uses what and can overview the domains.
	IT	If IT is the owner of the services, it is logical that the service portfolio is managed there.	It is strange that IT as the creator also decides on matters of business functionality.
Who manages the service portfolio with regard to design time?	Domain owners	Domain owner who feels responsible for the service portfolio.	Stands or falls by a good distinction between business domains. Risk of overlapping.
	Central organ	One central place where all service contracts are managed.	

Basic choice	Alternatives	Advantages	Disadvantages
Who manages the service portfolio with regard to runtime?	Domain owners	Domain owner who feels responsible for supplying the service.	Domain owners must regulate management and supervision for themselves.
	Central organ	One central place where the delivery of all services is monitored.	
Who is the owner of a service to be supplied?	Business	The business requests and defines functionalities in terms of services that have to be delivered by other business components; then it is logical that the business is the owner of the services. Fits in with the ownership of applications in the business.	Requires a clear division of the business into domains and the assignation of services.
	IT	IT searches for possibilities for reuse and combines identical functionalities in services that they supply to the business; then it is logical that IT is the owner of the functional building blocks.	IT cannot decide on its own about the reuse of functionalities in the business.
Choice for domains	Business units	Conformance to existing structures.	Risk that current silos continue to exist. Risk of overlapping in services.
	Functional areas: e.g. business functions	Pure division functional areas that are as autonomous as possible.	Functional structure that does not match the existing organizational structure.
How are services funded?	Projects	In general, fits in with existing funding constructions.	Projects are more expensive than normal because they have to take into account the reusability aspect.
	From central budget	Provides motivation to arrive at reusable services. More chance of success for SOA initiatives.	Must be regulated. Improper funding from central budget.
How is the use of services calculated and settled?	Depending on use	Fair division of the load.	Must be regulated.
	Not at all	No administration for recalculation of costs.	

Table 9.1 Basic choices for SOA implementation

Choosing business projects

The implementation of SOA takes place mainly in business projects, where the majority of the services are identified, designed, and implemented. Figure 9.1 shows that the first business projects are based on the so-called 'Entry Points', which are characteristic projects set up to deliver parts of the SOA infrastructure, and also to add direct value for the business by providing functionality in the form of potentially reusable services.

> **Examples of business projects that lend themselves to the application of SOA**
> - Increasing the productivity of call center staff.
> - Accelerating the throughput time of the order-processing method.
> - Implementing a new way of Customer Relationship Management.
> - Improving management information for senior management.

Finding the perfect pilot project can be a balancing act between risk and reward. The global risk of the project must be low enough to allow you to take the first steps towards SOA in serene fashion, and the awaited results significant enough to give the initiative visibility.

The risks must be kept low in order to maximize the probability of finishing on time, within the budget, without any cuts in the functional scope: a failure could threaten the SOA momentum. Mission critical projects whose delay could compromise some core business operations should, of course, be avoided.

A good pilot project is a quick win needing only a small budget allocation, which can be finished in a short timeframe. This requires a well-defined limited scope and no technical challenge to face. Actually, a SOA pilot project is not a proof of technology.

Gartner [Gartner 2006e] defines a 'sweet spot' for SOA pilot project candidates as an area in an IT complexity / Business value quadrant where the IT complexity is below average but business value is high (see Figure 9.2).

This business value is always directly related to business pain, which abounds in any organization. It must be quantifiable by one or two numeric metrics that every stakeholder must be able to understand and agree upon. The ROI of the project will be calculated on the basis of the value of those metrics, measured before and after the project. The business value of the project must be carefully evaluated: if it is too low, the project will lose the attention of its management sponsors and be considered as anecdotic, worthless.

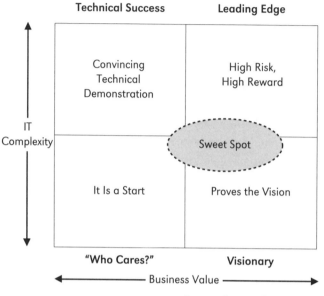

Source: Gartner (August 2006)

Figure 9.2 Sweet spot for SOA pilot project candidates

How SOA prevented fraud in restaurants

An international resort including hotels and restaurants had a very specific issue with one of their business processes. The clients who bought a package (hotel and meals) were given tickets with a barcode identifier allowing them to have their meals in the resort's restaurants. One ticket per meal and per person was provided. These tickets were collected and registered with a barcode reader at the entrance by a waiter.

Some time after this process was put in place, the consolidation of the results of the different restaurants of the resort showed that some tickets were used twice in the same day. The problem continued and led to a substantial loss of profit. The investigations brought to light that some staff members photocopied the tickets before giving them to the clients, using the duplicates for free meals.

The company started a project that enabled the use of the tickets to be controlled in real time. The architecture of the information system was modified and a set of shared services implemented so that the restaurant's ticket registration system could refuse the ticket if it had already been used once. This kind of fraud was eliminated and the company stopped losing money.

There are various possibilities for choosing business projects:

- Check which business projects are in the pipeline and designate certain projects as possible candidates for SOA (bottom-up approach).
- Identify promising application areas for SOA and initiate projects for this (bottom-up approach).
- Determine which business domains are most suitable to SOA on the basis of a business domain division, and initiate projects for these (middle-out approach).
- Generate a translation to a SOA-based enterprise architecture on the basis of the business strategy, and realize this via projects (top-down approach).

The possibility that suits you best is largely determined by the culture of your organization and the way in which changes are initiated. A top-down approach will be chosen in a strong hierarchical structure, but a bottom-up approach is more suitable in a more informal culture.

Choosing readiness projects

As shown in Figure 9.1, in addition to business projects, so-called 'readiness projects' can also be identified. These are projects aimed at preparing your organization for the efficient and effective application of SOA. These readiness projects issue from assessment with the SOA Maturity Model, and refer to the improvement of processes, particularly in the field of Enterprise Governance and Enterprise Architecture, by educating and making people aware, and choosing the appropriate technology.

Examples of readiness projects
- Describing roles and responsibilities with regard to the Service Life Cycle.
- Laying out a SOA Center of Excellence.
- Laying out Service Portfolio Management.
- Formulating standards and guidelines for the design of services. An important element in this is the guideline for the granularity of a service.
- Formulating SOA principles as a component of the enterprise architecture.
- Training business analysts and software engineers.
- Choosing and implementing a tool for the registration and retrieval of services.
- Laying out a development path for the assembly of services.
- Organizing a roadshow to communicate the concepts and added value of SOA for the organization to various target groups.
- Building a component bank (in order to manage IT assets but also business processes, design patterns, design guidelines, etc.)

SOA leads to more generic IT infrastructure. The SOA reference architecture in Chapter 4 describes 11 areas for which infrastructural aids are necessary. This generic SOA infrastructure is partly generated via business projects and partly via readiness projects. Implementing an Enterprise Service Bus (ESB) is a typical example of a readiness project. Most organizations find it terribly difficult to make a business case for an ESB, let alone find a sponsor in the business. Nevertheless, an ESB is of great importance as a transport and routing mechanism in SOA. As the SOA Maturity Model indicates, investment in technology is necessary at a given moment in order to prepare the organization for working with SOA. At first, business projects and readiness projects will fill in parts of the generic SOA infrastructure, but as time passes, it will be mainly business projects that benefit from the fact that there is an increasing amount of infrastructure that they can make use of. This considerably speeds up the business projects.

Ultimately, the SOA Roadmap consists of business and readiness projects. Because it is impossible to predict all SOA projects in advance, we advise you to formulate a roadmap for a certain period, preferably for a short period of around 6 months but not longer than 1 year. After this period, it is advisable to check your aims once again and to make a new assessment in order to formulate a new roadmap for a new period.

9.3 Entry points

The use of entry points (People, Information, Process, Reuse, and Connectivity) provides an answer to the question concerning the areas in which SOA can be implemented in an organization [IBM 2006a]. These entry points describe frequently recurring problems that can be solved with the aid of SOA. A project plan can be drawn up for each of the entry points. This type of project is not essentially different from any other project: there should be a concrete business aim supported by a business case. The value of the entry points lies primarily in the determination of a clear aim for the SOA project. What is the business problem that is to be solved with the introduction of SOA?

In partnership with Mercer Management Consulting, IBM has studied emerging practices among its 1,900 SOA clients. This research illuminated three core business-centric SOA starting points: People, Processes and

Information, and two IT-centric SOA starting points: Connectivity and Reuse.

A business-centric approach to SOA begins with the analysis of a business, in order to discover the areas which will most quickly benefit from improved access and integration by people in critical business areas. Through business-centric SOA, organizations can tie IT-related projects to the business need, directly addressing the immediate pain points of the company.

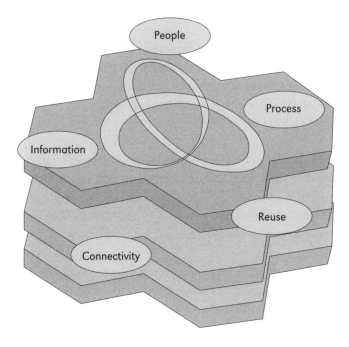

Figure 9.3 Five entry points

The SOA entry points help organizations pursue SOA the right way, by taking a project-based approach and demanding that each project deliver real business value, so that a business is ready to leverage the benefits of a SOA, understand the benefits of modular components and web services, enhance business processes, and seize new opportunities for improvement.

The entry points approach starts with the fundamental assets of an enterprise: People, Information and Processes from a business perspective. The technical groundwork for integration of People, Information and Processes will be delivered through the entry points for Connectivity and Reuse.

In the next few sections, we present short descriptions and examples per entry point as a result of real client engagements and experiences. We give insights into the business challenge, the entry point used, a short explanation of the solution, and what the real business benefits were. With this information you can recognize some of your own business challenges, which will give you guidance on what steps you can take.

9.3.1 People-centric collaboration

Starting the journey using a business-centric approach to SOA begins with the analysis of a business in order to discover the areas which will most quickly benefit from improved access and interaction by people in critical business areas. This entry point has everything to do with productivity through collaboration.

Companies that focus on collaboration among people are interested in improving their productivity by giving their employees, customers and partners the ability to create a personalized way in which to interact with other people and information, in the context of business processes. This enables human and process interaction with consistent levels of service.

Where do I start? You should start with targeted pilot projects that give the basic elements for expanding (SOA) solution areas, focusing on including user interaction through portals and dashboards. Build a view of key business processes by aggregating information to help people make better decisions. The next step will be a tighter management of performance with alert-driven dashboards that link to more processes.

Operational efficiency, the ability to innovate on the fly, and employee productivity are paramount to competitiveness and business growth. Organizations are currently struggling with silo-based applications and information that prevents employees, partners and customers working together efficiently. Empowering people enabled through service oriented solutions can bridge these challenges and provide a clear foundation for improved productivity, collaboration, and communication.

It is evident that people drive the interaction with the SOA services that execute business results. Therefore, focusing on people is critical to the success of SOA implementations.

Using the People entry point can help:
- Accelerate productivity.
- Reduce the cost of access to multiple application and information sources.
- Enable and improve collaboration inside and outside the enterprise.
- Reduce time to market, create deployment of new services.
- Increase access to process flexibility and orchestration.

As a complement to the other entry points of Process, Information, Reuse and Connectivity, this entry point can facilitate real-time decision making, dynamic collaboration, and immediate execution.

Clearly, the People entry point approach to SOA drives business and operational flexibility and improves productivity and collaboration. However, the proof of the pudding is in the eating. In the next example, we shall summarize a real client situation using the People entry point as the starting point for showing real business benefits.

People-centric collaboration at a conglomerate of schools

Introduction
The object is a large conglomerate of public elementary, middle, high schools and education centers with tens of thousands of multi-language students, teachers, administrators, public organizations, and parents (more than 200 colleges, universities, technical institutes, and military academies).
Close cooperation between these organizations, access to information, data sources, delivery of reports, and key performance indicators are of the utmost importance in delivering high-quality education to students.
However, they had relevant data sources spread over more than 300 siloed application environments which were poorly integrated, did not use any agreed technology standard, and lacked any architectural approach. Their business processes and the above mentioned IT environments were not aligned, resulting in weak collaboration, communication, and no reuse of any existing asset to lower the costs of development.

Business challenge
The challenge was to create a single access point for all people involved in improving collaboration and communication, and to improve students' performances, increase the overall quality of education, improve information access for more than 2,000 administrators, and quickly respond to deficiencies in order to comply with public

legislation, as is obligatory for schools receiving public funding. If they are not able to deliver well-substantiated reports, it puts the funding in jeopardy.

Furthermore, there should be improved alignment between the business processes and IT environment, using existing assets connected through open standards as much as possible, independent of proprietary solutions.

Solution

After the business, functional and nonfunctional requirements analysis, a SOA blueprint was delivered, integrating the disparate IT environments into a role-based portal. Students, teachers, administrators, parents, and external public organizations have 7 * 24-hour access to applications, information, and services.

The 2,000 administrators leverage the portal environment, monitoring school resources, generating reports and tracking student attendance, grades and assessments. This now enables them to correlate business factors, *i.e.*, the amount of money spent per student, the average score per school, attendance score cards, etc.

Teachers can access student data and students will be able to access class assignments, student resources and calendars, and communicate with their teachers and peers. The environment can be deployed in multiple languages for improved communications.

Some of the disparate applications have been integrated after some componentization, using web services, preserving existing assets, and avoiding becoming locked into proprietary solutions.

Business benefits

The real business benefits lie in the collaboration between the teachers, students, administrators, and external organizations. This shows a significant improvement. Besides this, administrators are now able to generate reports in minutes instead of weeks, enabling faster awareness of, and response to, performance problems.

The applications and related data sources, formerly separated, can now be accessed through one interface, thus improving insight into performance district-wide and expanding resources for all parties involved.

The ability to track student performance will help increase test scores, ensuring compliance with public legislation. As a direct effect, funding is no longer in jeopardy.

9.3.2 Business process management

Organizations with a business process management focus are interested in the ability to optimize their processes, deploying them quickly when necessary, and monitoring the effectiveness of the altered processes. As a consequence, they are able to react to changing market demands better and to act accordingly. However, an organization needs to ensure that the process components are completely reusable so that they can be reconfigured quickly and efficiently.

Do your business processes allow you to respond quickly to changing market conditions? By streamlining business processes you are able to align business and IT objectives and reduce the complexity of building processes.

Start by modeling an underperforming process, remove the bottlenecks, then simulate and deploy the optimized process. The next step could be to create flexible links between multiple processes across the enterprise, and bridge the gap between customers, suppliers, and partners. Finally, monitor the process according to well substantiated Key Performance Indicators, and track the performance.

Leveraging SOA with focus on the process entry point can help to:
- Increase collaboration with partners and suppliers.
- Accelerate the time to market.
- Respond quickly to business challenges and act accordingly.
- Implement new processes faster.
- Respond better to compliancy regulations.
- Maximize return on investment.

Business process management at a motorcycle manufacturer

Introduction
A motorcycle manufacturer recognized and respected throughout the world has a lot of enthusiastic owners wishing to keep their own identity. It is a vital company that tries to expand its product portfolio by reacting to market demand, taking into account specific regional customer requirements and investigating the market capabilities for expanding business.
It has established good cooperation between its own organization and its suppliers, dealers, customers and investors, and understands the real importance of marketing and providing specialized services around its products.
Down through the years, information technology has become very important, not only in supporting business processes but also as a differentiator that does more for its dealer organization and customers.

Business challenge

The company understands the importance of business model innovation which can help to reduce costs and improve profitability. In the current competitive market, it needs a flexible and agile financial system that is able to react swiftly to the successful outcome of a marketing campaign.

However, the application architecture was tightly coupled using outdated technology. There was no integrated choreography between credit applications, credit approvals, and loan origination. Changing the functionality in the separate applications cost a lot of time, money and effort, but did not deliver with regard to the demands of the marketing promotion programmes. Because of this, the company was losing important market momentum, which required a swift solution.

Solution

The company started with the architectural blueprint of the financial domain from a business perspective by drawing up financial package process models. This enabled it to innovate its business processes to support and promote financial plans to the retail channels, like the dealers.

The application domain was re-architected in line with SOA guidelines and principles, and the company used a SOA that disconnected the hardwired integrated application domain and changed it into services that are now independent and loosely coupled. As a result, the financial domain is now web-based and its credit approval process application can provide new necessary financial programmes that react swiftly to marketing demands. New and existing functionality can be modified quickly and has the ability to change without interfering with the components of other services.

Business benefits

The following improvements have been gained:
- Financial programmes that can be cheaply mapped to marketing promotions on the fly.
- New assortments can be brought to the marketplace faster when required.
- The services component is only modified when relevant, not touching every functionality.
- Customer services have been improved by developing financing strategies more quickly and in full alignment with customer needs.

9.3.3 Information as a service

Information as a service is an entry point to SOA that offers information access to complex, heterogeneous data sources within a company as reusable services. These services may be available within an organization or across a value chain. Enterprises focused on information as a service are very interested in the ability to improve their business insights, reducing risk by using trusted information services delivered in line and in context.

But, as information becomes of key significance to every organization, duplicate or contradictory information needs to be avoided, because users have to be able to 'trust' the information. By going into SOA via this entry point, it is possible to improve the ability and consistency of information, and to breakdown traditional barriers to information sharing.

Do you have a clear understanding about your company's information sources and relationships? Do you know the exact added value of information to your business? Then it is time to establish information as a service, ensuring consistent definitions, packaging, and governance of important business data, with the objective of being able to provide information services that can simply be reused across your business processes. This will enable more business flexibility while at the same time improving the productivity of IT because the services can be independently maintained.

One can start by discovering and understanding information sources, relationships, and the business context. The next step will be to expand the volume and scope of the information delivered as a service across internal and external processes. This entry point can add value to SOA through information, by;

- Increasing an organization's agility; by providing reusable information services, bridging structured and unstructured information that can be connected into applications, business processes, and/or portals. Through this development, the costs associated with accessing and transforming data can be reduced.
- Making data accessible; develop a unified view of the business with clear integration of analytical data for improved transparency and business insight.
- Reducing cost and risk associated with infrastructure rationalization and migration by disconnecting information from the previously mentioned siloed application environments. Reduce risk by means of inline analytics and auditable data quality for risk and compliancy initiatives from internal and external organizational bodies.

Starting separate projects from the People, Process or Information entry points will deliver benefits, while also offering the potential of delivering optimized return on investment. However, combining the three SOA entry points from a business perspective in one well-orchestrated effort can deliver benefits even faster.

Nonetheless, without information technology, it is impossible to integrate the People, Processes, and Information within a business. Experience shows that service oriented infrastructure is required, consisting of a self-secured, self-healing, self-configuring and self-optimizing standardized communication layer which supports the transformation from a vertical, siloed, application-driven infrastructure into a more horizontal driven approach.

Information as a service at a telecommunication provider

Introduction
Through its multi-million customer connections, this large telecommunication provider delivers comprehensive and innovative suites of communication services to residential and business customers in different parts of the world.
The company provides consumers with simple solutions to all their communication needs, including telephone services, wireless, high-speed Internet, digital television satellite communication, and voice over IP. Besides this, it offers information and communications technology solutions to leading large enterprises, small and medium-sized businesses, and public sector organizations.

Business challenge
The company needed to act upon competitive and regulatory external pressures associated with the telecom industry. Knowing the fierce competition, it had to improve its understanding of its customers and the relationship with them.
Because of the limited customer loyalty in the telecom business, it also needed to offer innovative products to their customers, which forced it to change its thinking from a product-centric perspective to a customer-centric perspective. To make this turnaround successful, it needed to identify the most profitable customers, create a single view of those customers across applications and line of businesses, and improve customer loyalty as much as possible.

Solution
A well-substantiated standardized data model for the whole company was an essential building block and the starting point of its SOA journey. To solve this problem, a

new customer system was implemented, using master data integration technology. This was aligned with the quality rules from its existing data warehouse implementation, creating a single holistic view of customers across multiple operational systems.

Business benefits
By creating a solution from this SOA entry point, this company improved its target marketing success by being able to identify and link customers across different channels. Rapid identification and classification of customers was possible, resulting in offers that accurately represent segment and customer profile. Additionally, changes in government regulations can now be dealt with even faster.
As a direct effect, the enhanced customer experience increased loyalty and significantly reduced 'churn'. The administration costs were reduced through improved efficiency, and the ability to reuse information as a service delivered a huge reduction on the costs of interfaces (only 2.5% of the cost compared to the first implemented interface).

9.3.4 Connectivity

The connectivity entry point helps the organization integrate the business-centric SOA entry points. Connectivity has always been an important requirement in the past and will even be more important for SOA implementations in the future. It is designed to simplify the IT environment with a more secure, reliable and scalable way to connect within and beyond the business. It should interlink people, information and processes using flows of messages and information from virtually any place, any time, and from any source. This is where the connectivity domain really adds value. Delivering real business value on its own, connectivity is also a core building block for near future SOA initiatives.

The establishment of an Enterprise Service Bus (ESB) could be part of the connectivity entry point. It is a collection of middleware that unifies and connects services, applications, and resources within a business. Put another way, it is the framework within which the capabilities of a business's applications are made available for reuse by other applications throughout the organization and even beyond its boundaries.

What is the value of service connectivity for your organization? It can open the doors for customers, partners and suppliers, providing them with a variety of ways to interact with your enterprise. By enabling connectivity, one can deliver a consistent presentation logic regardless of which business channel is chosen. Integrating business units and/or divisions internally and externally will produce improved collaboration.

In summary, the connectivity entry point can help:
- Integrate the people, process and information domain.
- Scale a business fully aligned with market growth.
- Build trusted relationships with customers, suppliers, and partners.
- Create a scalable, secured and available connection domain using open standards.

Connectivity at a water technology solutions provider

Introduction
Making plumbing fixtures functional as well as attractive is the overriding goal of this company, a water technology solutions provider in Europe, and also the largest exporter of faucets, bath mountings, and other household and commercial fittings worldwide.

The company delivers products and additional services in more than 100 countries through business partners spread all over the world. Export sales comprise around 80 per cent of the total business and are therefore crucial in building incremental business.

Business challenge
The speed of delivery of new products is very important in this marketplace because competition is fierce. A head start in this market will usually result in increased sales. However, the application environment supporting the existing plant operations, business processes and logistic systems is not well integrated. Custom coding for new and updated business applications slowed the time to market and raised the costs.

In gathering requirements for a new ERP (enterprise resource planning) system, the company had to figure out how to exchange data between the new ERP modules and several legacy applications. These included duty and plant applications and delivery, invoice and product catalogue systems, as well as bar coding, logistics and inventory management software.

In total, the company identified 14 interfaces that needed to be created. As the project had to be completed quickly, the company needed to determine whether it was more cost effective to perform hand-coded, point-to-point integration or purchase a packaged solution designed for speedy integration and continued consistency of business processes. Vendor lock-in had also to be avoided.

Solution
The existing plant operations, business processes and logistic systems were integrated using an Enterprise Service Bus (ESB) environment enabling the integration of back-end systems and databases. Passing and transforming between 5,000 and 25,000 messages per day, the Enterprise Service Bus solution enables a global exchange of information with a string of services between loosely coupled front and back ends.

Business benefits
The real business benefits lie in the improved integration of business, people and processes and full business alignment with export market revenue growth.

The average integration time decreased by up to 84% (two to four weeks versus up to six months); furthermore the time and cost for integrating legacy applications with new ERP modules were reduced, compared to a hand-coded, point-to-point integration technique.

The solution also brought more reliable and highly available data transfers: service-enabling legacy systems for the reuse of assets on demand. Using this approach, the company estimates that its IT group can bring a new service online within two to four weeks. This will help improve time-to-market significantly.

9.3.5 Reuse

Building reusable components means creating (a specific set of) functions and supplying the standard interfaces that allow them to be used over and over again.

The primary goal for every SOA implementation is to maximize reuse at each existing IT layer. This can be done by refactoring redundant capabilities, exposing and promoting common functionality, and composing new business relevant functions as reusable services. This can only be achieved by introducing strong SOA Governance focused on measures that promote reuse to reduce IT costs and time-to-market for competitive advantage.

It is essential to cut costs, reduce development cycle times, and expand access to core applications through reuse. Reuse gives users flexibility through reduced cycle times and by eliminating duplicate processes.

As a starting point, one can use portfolio management to consider which IT assets are needed to run a company. Next, it is essential to identify important, high value existing IT assets and enable them for reuse. The remaining business needs can be delivered through creating new services. A registry and repository providing centralized access and control of these new and reusable assets will also be beneficial in this approach.

What value can reuse bring to an organization?
- It lowers maintenance costs by eliminating redundant systems.
- It reduces the amount of new code that must be created for business initiatives.
- There is less disinvestment of current IT environment.
- New business functions can be created by composite functions from existing applications.

Reuse at a large bank

Introduction
A large bank provides commercial banking services to a diverse customer base that includes large corporations, small and medium-sized businesses, and consumers. The bank's 9000 employees deliver financial products and services through a nationwide network of nearly 250 branches, more than 1000 ATMs and additional electronic distribution channels.

Business challenge
Around the world, banks are finding that they must improve the way they do business in order to survive in fiercely competitive markets. The old ways of doing business just won't work. Banks are competing with insurance companies and brokerages that are providing banking services. International banks are fighting for local business. Banks are differentiating themselves from competitors by finding new ways to serve customers better, because these customers are switching to banks that offer new services and greater convenience. To improve its competitive positioning, the bank needed to take action.

Emphasis was put on doing simplified business through multiple channels reusing existing assets and applications (CRM, Web, else) as much as possible.

Furthermore, competitiveness had to be enhanced by enabling a faster, simpler and more flexible infrastructure that would support new business processes targeted at improving customer service for consumers.

Solution

After a well-defined business requirements analysis (functional and nonfunctional), existing application functions were reused and transformed into business services by using XML. Business and functional modeling tools were used, redefining some business processes and using existing assets as much as possible. By doing this, old code could be reused and the development time could be reduced by 40%.

Older applications, such as Internet banking, still met the performance requirements, although they were accessing some of the same sources as the CRM, ERP and core banking systems. With its new SOA-enabled architecture, the bank was able to implement reusable services offered by new applications, such as credit risk scoring and operations identity, without affecting its existing Web architecture.

Business benefits

By reusing existing assets and optimizing the IT environment, the average monthly transaction rate of the bank increased by 300%, due to simplified bank access for customers using multiple channels. The bank was able to respond better to market change and customer requirements. Customer intimacy increased significantly by means of improved perceived customer services.

The reuse of nearly 51% of existing services reduced application development time and maintenance costs, resulting in millions of dollars in savings. Improved response time to changing business requirements could be realized by a flexible application infrastructure that enabled the bank's IT staff to focus on other line-of-business requirements, improving overall service while reducing the need to hire and train additional personnel.

9.4 Summary

So, how do I travel the SOA road and what makes sense for my organization? As already explained, there is no standard way, it depends largely on your business priorities, scope, and objectives. However, taking a business-centric approach to SOA will help your organization ensure that you are keeping your investment focused on areas that mean the most to your common line. Starting with the Strategic Dialogue and creating a SOA Roadmap will help you to determine your priorities and objectives for your SOA journey. The key elements of such a roadmap are certain business projects and certain readiness projects. Entry Points will help you in finding the right business projects to start with, by identifying the corresponding business benefits.

Because it is impossible to predict all SOA projects in advance, it is advisable to formulate the roadmap for a certain period, preferably between 6 and 12 months. After this period you can make up your mind again, check your aims, do an assessment with the SOA Maturity Model, and draw up a new roadmap for a new period.

10 Safely reaching your destination

10.1 Introduction

As seen in the previous chapters, implementing SOA is not something to underestimate. The sheer complexity of all the services and business processes to be built, delivered, implemented, or used by all kinds of internal or external parties can be a major challenge. In fact, the path to our destination is strewn with risks. If these risks are insufficiently dealt with, we may end up somewhere, but not at the original destination in mind – or the original destination may be reached weeks or months too late or at a cost that is simply much too high.

When talking about the risks that litter the path to our destination, two types of risks can be identified:
- Risks related to the process of getting to the destination. These could be risks such as 'the implementation must go live on 1 January'; or 'specifications are delivered late', 'skilled testers are not available', or 'the infrastructure is not ready in time'.
- Risks related to the destination of the journey itself – in other words, risk related to SOA.

What if this architecture fails or has errors in it? This would result in big risks to the company's operations, risks such as: high rework costs, loss of productivity, brand/reputation damage. The consequences may include compensation claims perhaps, and the loss of competitiveness through the late availability of a new product or service (leading to a revenue loss).

Before an organization starts using SOA, it should explicitly ask itself whether all the requirements have been met. Have all the services, sub systems, objects, and the architecture called for in the requirements been explored to sufficient depth? Besides functionality, have checks been carried out, for example, on effectiveness, performance and security? Has it been established whether the SOA possesses the characteristics and features necessary to meet the stated or (even more difficult) implied needs? It is important to note that what may appear as self-evident to one person may be a revelation to another.

The real question is: what risks are being taken and which measures have been taken to mitigate those risks. To avoid obtaining answers to such crucial questions only during the operational phase of the SOA, a good, reliable testing process is required in advance of going operational. That demands, in turn, that a structured approach be taken to testing, to the organization and infrastructure, with which continuous insight may be obtained (in a controlled manner) into the status of SOA and its associated risks. These challenges are somewhat different compared to 'traditional' software development and can be summarized in four statements. These statements are introduced here and explained in a more detailed way in the next chapter.

Who owns, who pays?

When a service is used in more than one service or business process, the quality must be excellent. To test this type of service, it is necessary to put in additional test effort. The question is, who is going to pay for this? The department delivering the service or the department using it? So this leads to the question as to who benefits most from a high-quality service and who's prepared to pay for it. When answering this it's necessary to bear in mind that testing prevents (high) reworking costs and consequential damage to the complete SOA, thanks to defects found during testing and rectified within the system development process. It also adds to faith in the complete SOA.

When to test which service?

In SOA, the services are related to one another in a structured way. One service can deliver the input for another service, for example, and vice versa. This sometimes means that to test one service you need another service. But is this service already available, already tested, and good enough? When testing SOA you have to align the planning of this test with the planning of the development or implementation of the services, because you cannot test before the required service has been adequately developed.

How to test a service?

Most of the services in SOA do not have a user interface. Most of the testers are accustomed to testing something with a user interface. These two facts combined describe a big problem that has to be faced when testing SOA. Something is needed to communicate with the service.

A lot of services, a lot of testing

With all these services going on, the risk is there that the test team will want to test everything on every level. Many test levels and types exist, like the prototype test, the unit test, the unit integration test, the unit regression test, the service test, the service integration test, the service regression test, the service performance test, the system test, the system integration test. It is not possible to test everything. Therefore you have to make a choice, based on risks and priorities.

To meet these challenges, a structured test approach is needed. This type of approach is typified by:

- Providing a structure, so that it is exactly clear *what*, by *whom*, *when* and in *which sequence* things have to be done.
- Covering the full scope and describing the complete range of relevant activities.
- Providing a solid foundation for the future, so that the proverbial testing 'wheel' doesn't have to be reinvented over and over again.
- Managing test activities in the context of available time, money, and quality.

TMap is Sogeti's internationally recognised test approach [Koomen 2006]. This approach can be summarized with four essentials.

1. TMap is based on a business-driven test management (BDTM) approach.
2. TMap describes a structured test process.
3. TMap contains a complete tool kit.
4. TMap is an adaptive test method.

The first essential can be related directly to the fact that the business case of IT is important to organizations. The BDTM approach provides content that addresses this fact in TMap and can therefore be seen as the 'leading thread' of the structured TMap test process (the second essential). The TMap life cycle model is used in the description of the test process. Furthermore, various aspects in the field of infrastructure, techniques and organization must be set up to execute the test process correctly. TMap provides much practical applicable information on this, in the form of examples, checklists, technique descriptions, procedures, test organization structures, test environments, and test tools (third essential). TMap also has a flexible set-up so that it can be implemented in different system development situations: for new development and the maintenance of a system, for a self-developed system or an acquired package, and for outsourcing (parts of) the testing process. In other words, TMap is an adaptive method (fourth essential).

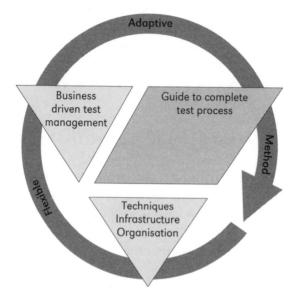

Figure 10.1 TMap model of essentials

10.2 Defining a SOA testing strategy

How can we set up testing so that it covers the important risks to SOA implementation? And more importantly, what are these risks? This set-up is performed in a process with several steps and requires the involvement of testers, consumer(s) of the service(s), and other stakeholders.

The key to testing is that you test what needs to be tested, and just enough to cover the risk. Tests are executed on the basis of test cases, checklists, and the like. But what kind of tests are they? To ensure the tests' usefulness, they must be set up to test *those* characteristics and parts of a service (or combination of services) that represent a risk if the service does not function adequately in production later on. This means that various considerations have already been made before test execution can begin. In other words, some thought has already been given to which parts of the service need not be tested, and which parts must be tested and how and with what coverage. So what determines this? Why not test all parts of the service as thoroughly as possible? If an organization possessed unlimited resources, one option might indeed be to test everything as thoroughly as possible. But naturally, in real life, an organization never has the resources to actually do this, which means that choices must be made regarding what is tested and how thoroughly. One of the seven easy concepts of SOA is an economic one and therefore such choices are also economic. If you spend money on SOA, you will want to know what you are getting in return. The theory of IT Governance controls SOA projects on the basis of four aspects: *result, risk, time,* and *cost*. For instance, it might be a more attractive investment for an organization to start a high risk SOA project that potentially yields a high result than a SOA project with very low risks where the benefits barely exceed the costs.

When testing SOA, this economic justification of IT plays an important role and it must be translated into the activity of testing. For the successful execution of a project, it is important that the test process is aligned with the four IT Governance aspects described above. The relationship between these aspects is made via the business-driven test management (BDTM) approach. An outline of this approach is given below, with specific focus on testing in SOA.

10.3 The steps in the business-driven test management approach

To understand the BDTM approach, it is important to keep an eye on the final objective, which is to provide a quality assessment and risk recommendation about the service. Since not everything can be tested, a correct assessment can only be realized by dividing the test effort, in terms of time and money, as adequately as possible over parts and characteristics of the service to be tested. The person to make the ultimate decision on the balance between the time and cost to be expended on testing, versus results to be achieved and risks to be covered with testing, is the client. To be able to make this decision in a well-founded way, the test manager needs to involve the client in the process and supply the right information. In the figure below, the client is therefore placed in a central role.

The steps that make up the BDTM approach are explained below in the next three sections.

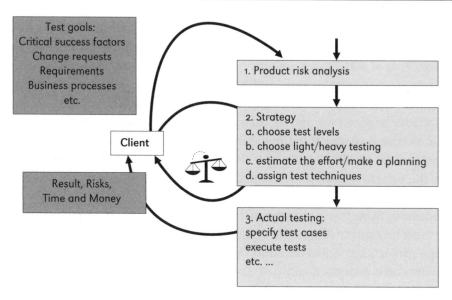

Figure 10.2 BDTM steps

10.3.1 Performing a product risk analysis

In a product risk analysis, the service or business process to be tested is ana-lysed with the aim of achieving a joint view – for the test manager and other stakeholders – of the greater or lesser risk-bearing features and parts of the service(s) or business process to be tested, so that the thoroughness of testing can be related to this view.

The focus in product risk analysis is on the product risks, *i.e.*, what is the risk to the organization if the product does not have the expected quality, and is this risk low, medium, or (very) high?

A product risk is the chance that the product will fail in relation to the expected damage if this occurs.

In practice, a non-exhaustive list of typical product risks specific to SOA envi-ronments is:

* A service is of insufficient quality for the one or more other services or business processes that make use of it, resulting in a defective cluster of services where the cause of a defect is hard to find.

- The service can be of sufficient quality for the business process it was designed for in the first place, but is it also of sufficient quality for use in other business processes?
- The services don't conform to the architectural standards, resulting in inflexible IT with many overlapping services.
- There's too much focus on functionality, ignoring other requirements, resulting in poor performance or lack of security, for instance.
- The services and business processes are insufficiently aligned, resulting in ineffective and inefficient business processes.

These risks are, amongst many other things, also dependent on the maturity of the SOA implementation, ranging from just having an Enterprise Service Bus connecting legacy applications, up to full-blown SOA with business services supporting the business processes.

Assessing product risks is a complex task. You need to have knowledge of (the risks of) the architecture, of individual technical and business services, of the business processes, and of possible damage and the chance of defects. The test manager does not possess this knowledge, or does so only to a limited extent. Moreover, the knowledge is usually distributed over various parties or people. Therefore the organization and client of the SOA are responsible for the correct assessment of the product risks. In practice, the test manager is usually the facilitator and organizer of the product risk analysis, approaching various people who can contribute knowledge about the product risks. Table 10.1 shows likely candidates to involve in the product risk analysis.

In addition to the fact that the product risk analysis serves as the basis for the test strategy, another advantage is that the various parties become more aware of both the risks and the consequences. A shared and widely supported image of the main risks with their classifications is created. In the rest of the testing process, this helps generate commitment if decisions must be made in the relevant field.

However, just brainstorming with a couple of people on product risks is unlikely to result in good risk coverage of all parts and aspects of the service(s) to be tested. The aim is not to think up as many product risks as possible, but to assess the risk for each part or aspect of the service.

Role	Focus	Expertise
Client of the business service, usually the manager responsible for the business process	Damage (if it goes wrong, what is the damage?)	Business processes
Enterprise architect	Chance of failure (what are the error-prone areas of the SOA or service?)	Architecture
Owner of individual (technical or business) service	Chance of failure / damage	Business and technical service
Business analyst	Damage	Business processes, business service
Senior user	Damage	Business process, business service
Developer	Chance of failure	Business and technical service
Project manager	Damage/chance of failure	All areas
Quality Assurance	Chance of failure	All areas
(Functional and system) administrator	Damage	All areas
Requirements manager	Damage/chance of failure	Business and technical service

Table 10.1 Likely candidates for participating in the product risk analysis

As the product risk analysis is primarily a tool for communication, a good way to start is from the point of view of the SOA client and other acceptants, *i.e.*, from the perspective of what they believe to be important. These are called the 'test goals'. A test goal is a goal for testing relevant to the client, often formulated in terms of IT-supported business processes (ordering, invoicing), user requirements or use cases to be implemented, critical success factors, change proposals, or defined risks to be covered.

For each test goal, the participants then determine the relevant quality characteristics. In other words, which aspects should the test work cover in order to be able to achieve the test goals? In most cases, the characteristic of 'functionality' or 'correctness' is a relevant one. The test manager must make clear that other characteristics, such as performance, user-friendliness and security, can also be relevant for testing, depending on their risk. As an example, is performance an issue for the business process of 'Ordering'?

After selecting the relevant characteristics for testing each test goal, the characteristics are gathered together. The participants then split up the (business) service into a number of object parts (or components) for each characteristic. For Performance, these may be infrastructure, individual technical services, or the complete business service. For User-friendliness, these may be data entry screens or data view screens. For Functionality, these may be the Enterprise Service Bus or technical services. But the business service is usually also split up into different parts, such as functional parts for customers, orders, invoices, and management information, for instance.

The division into object parts makes it possible to make more refinements later when selecting the test coverage. The participants give the object parts a risk class, from low to very high, taking into account the risk of the object part in relation to achieving the test goals. An example is shown in Table 10.2.

Characteristic / Object part	Risk Class
Functionality	
• service 1	High
• service 2	Medium
• business service	Medium
User-friendliness	Medium
Performance	
• online	Medium
• batch	Low

Table 10.2 Risk assessment for quality characteristics and object parts of SOA

The result is incorporated in the (master) test plan and constitutes the basis for the subsequent decisions in the test strategy as to light, medium, thorough (or not) testing of a quality characteristic/object part of the SOA implementation.

10.3.2 Defining the test strategy

Defining the test strategy consists of four steps, as indicated in Figure 10.2. These steps will be explained below.

Choose test levels

A product risk analysis is performed with regard to the total test process for testing the (business) service. This usually involves *multiple* test levels. Conventional test levels are unit test, unit integration test, system test, and (user and/or production) acceptance test. It is first determined in a so-called master test plan which test levels must be set up. SOA testing usually requires another (extra) test level: the *service test*. The aim of this test level is to assess the quality of the individual (technical or lower-level business) services to be used in the business service. This prevents a big bang effect of all kinds of services being integrated into the business service, only to find that the service as a whole doesn't work (properly). If the quality of a service is too low, the individual service test is a far better instrument to assess this than in a system test of the total business service, where it's a lot more difficult to trace the cause of a defect to an underlying service.

For a service test, it doesn't really matter whether the services are bought, reused, or newly built. What does matter is the risk of a specific service. For a service that is bought, these risks usually differ from a service that is newly built. For instance, in an off-the-shelf service that is bought from a commercial vendor, you may expect to find very few functional defects compared to a newly built service. On the other hand, an in-house designed and developed service can be expected to have a better fit in the SOA. The product risk analysis should demonstrate these differences.

An important aspect in testing, but especially for testing in SOA environments, is the clarification of the responsibility for each test level. Is the vendor or supplier of a service responsible for the test level, is it the party demanding the service (IT), or the solution (business)? Especially in relation to the service test, this is not always clear. Our preference is to have the party using the service made responsible for the service test. This does not necessarily mean the party also has to perform the test: that may well be done by the supplier of the service, as long as the test results are reviewed by the user of the service.

Choose light/heavy testing

To determine the thoroughness of testing, the risk class per object part (from the product risk analysis) is used as a starting point. Initially, the following applies: the greater the risk, the more thorough the required testing. The result is recorded in a strategy table per test level; for an example, see Table 10.3.

Characteristic / Object part	Risk Class	Review	Development Test	Service Test	System Test	Acceptance Test
Functionality						
• service 1	High	●	● ●	● ● ●		
• service 2	Medium	●	●	● ●		
• business service	Medium	●		●	● ●	●
User-friendliness	Medium	●				● ●
Performance						
• online	Medium			●		● ●
• batch	Low					●

Table 10.3 Test strategy for each characteristic and object part

The Development Test in Table 10.3 consists of unit and unit integration tests. The System Test tests the integration of services. In the Acceptance Test, the business service will be tested.

An important test is the so-called 'regression test', which tests whether changes to the IT environment (in architecture, infrastructure, services, or business process for instance) have any unforeseen consequences in other parts. As many changes can be expected (after all, SOA is implemented to make the organization more flexible), this test forms the backbone for a good SOA test strategy and is often automated. Regression testing is performed in almost every test level.

A service often has no user interface. In order to test a service, a layer has to be built around the service, making it easy to invoke the service by means of a certain input, and to check the output of the service. This layer is called a harness. The development (and testing!) of these harnesses is something to take into account when planning the test.

Testing a (business) service requires business knowledge. (End) users have this knowledge, but are often scared by the technical environment of testing a service individually. Also, it's hard for a user to test a service in isolation, as the test data are often artificial and not production-like. Involving users in service testing requires good preparation, training and coaching.

A business service employing a variety of distributed services has to be tested both in isolation and in combination (integration) with other business services/systems. These tests, typically user acceptance tests, pose a major challenge to the organization in terms of the test environments (hardware, network, databases, test data) required. Setting up a representative, stable and production-like test environment requires a lot of coordination between various organizations, departments, and teams. It is very complex and often very expensive. Early involvement of people with knowledge of infrastructure and environments is key.

Estimate the effort and draw up a planning schedule
An overall estimate is then made for the test and a planning schedule is formulated. Especially with regard to SOA, it is crucial to test early in the developmental life cycle of a service. Early testing can demonstrate quality problems that are still fairly easy to repair at that moment, while later on, the costs of repair will rise considerably.

This is communicated to the client and other stakeholders and, depending on their views, adjusted as necessary. This gives the client control of the test process, enabling him to manage on the basis of the balance between result and risk, on the one hand, and time and cost, on the other.

The steps *Choose light/heavy testing* and *Estimate the effort and draw up a planning schedule* are repeated until the client is satisfied with the balance between estimated time and costs of testing on the one hand, and results to be achieved and risks to be covered on the other.

Assign test techniques
When the client and stakeholders agree on the strategy, estimate and the planning, the test manager translates the decisions concerning thorough and less thorough testing into concrete statements about how the testing should take place, and which techniques should be used to achieve the targeted coverage of a service, allocating test design techniques to the combinations of characteristic and object part. The available test basis, among other things, is taken into account. These techniques are used to design and execute the test cases (and/or checklists) at a later stage. This is where the primary test process starts.

The above activities are performed for the overall test process, the results are recorded in the master test plan. At the individual test level (unit test, service test, acceptance test), the activities are performed in more detail, if necessary.

10.3.3 Actual testing

After the plan(s) with the strategy have been approved, the actual testing (preparation, specification and execution of tests) starts. During testing, the test manager provides the client and other stakeholders with adequate insight into and control options over:
- The progress of the test process
- The quality and risks of the service(s) under test
- The quality of the test process.

10.4 Advantages of the business-driven test management approach

The above BDTM process for deciding on what to test and how thoroughly this is to be done stresses the importance of good communication between the testers and the stakeholders in the testing. BDTM starts from the principle that the selected test approach must enable the client to control the test process and (help) determine the test approach. This gives the testing a business-like and rational character. The required information to make this possible is delivered from the test process.

Business-driven test management has the following specific properties:
- The total test effort is related to the risks of the system to be tested for the organization. The deployment of people, resources and budget thereby focuses on those parts of the system that are most important to the organization.
- The estimate and planning for the test process are related to the defined test strategy. If there is an implementation of changes that have an impact on the thoroughness of testing for the various system parts or systems, this is translated immediately into a change in the estimate and/or planning. The organization is thus ensured of an adequate view of the required budget, lead time, and relationship with the test strategy at all times.
- The client is involved in making choices at various moments during the test process. The advantage is that the test process matches the wishes and requirements – and therefore the expectations – of the organization as adequately as possible.

Are we there yet? Unfortunately not. IT development is never a stable situation and SOA, in particular, is a highly flexible environment. Risks change, unexpected developments arise, new releases are pushed, modified services implemented, and so on. You should realize that a product risk analysis and test strategy are merely a snapshot in time. In the course of the subsequent process, it will be found that some risks have been overestimated and some have been underestimated or neglected altogether. The test manager must adjust the test strategy and the associated estimated effort, as well as the planning. Basically, the same steps as described above are followed to achieve this adjustment, only much more lightly. Again, this means that the client keeps a good grip on the test process and its results: adequate quality SOA.

10.5 The test environment when testing SOA

A fitting test environment is required to perform a dynamic test of SOA. Setting up and maintaining the test environment represents the introduction of expertise about which testers generally have no knowledge. This is why a separate department – outside the test project – is often responsible for setting up and maintaining the test environment. Testers are, however, heavily dependent on the test environment – no test can be executed without a test environment.

The set-up and composition of a test environment depends on the aim of the test. The success of a test environment depends on the determination of the extent to which the SOA or part of the architecture meets the requirements. Every test may have a different aim, which is why every test can use a different test environment. A test of one service, for instance, requires a completely different configuration of the test environment than an acceptance test of the complete SOA.

With SOA, an organization can use an increasing number of different types of hardware and software. When setting up a test environment for this type of architecture, this is translated into a chain of different hardware and software configurations with mutual interfaces. The metaphor 'the chain is as strong as its weakest link' then holds true. If one service or interface in the chain fails, the entire chain is useless and complete testing is impossible.

Organizing these test environments is a challenge, which, whatever the situation, the testers must face. Since the chains runs across multiple services, several departments are involved. Moreover, all components of the test environment must be completed at the same time, while arrangements must be made for the required test data in the various components.

To organize this properly, the various stakeholders have to be in agreement in advance of finalization of the master test plan. We recommend creating the role of 'chain coordinator' in the test organization. The chain coordinator is responsible for setting up and maintaining the test environment. While a test is being executed, the chain coordinator ensures that all parts of the chain are available, while acting as the primary point of contact for the various parties involved in the test.

When several projects use the same test environment, arrangements have to be made about the use of test data. This is the case when, for example, Project A executes tests using data from Service A, and Project B is required to modify this service. The situation might occur that Project A retrieves data from another version of the service in the afternoon than it did in the morning, which would, of course, affect the reliability of Project A's tests. To prevent this, it is advisable to make such instances the responsibility of the chain coordinator too. In conjunction with all the other parties involved, he or she will define a plan for defining and maintaining the test data.

10.6 Adaptation during SOA testing

One of the seven easy concepts of SOA focuses on change. The concept of 'Facilitate change, continually improve' describes how change is everywhere and how SOA can help react to this. It is often thought that testing and continuous changes are enemies. The general idea is that when you need to test thoroughly you need a stable product that will not change. Otherwise it will be very hard to test anything. This is not true.

As a tester you need the capability to adapt to changing situations and needs. This adaptability is more than just being able to respond to the changing environment. It is also being able to leverage changes for the benefit of testing. Being adaptive as a tester can be summarized in four properties of adaptability:

- Responsiveness to changes.
- Reuse of products and processes.
- Learn from experience.
- Try before use.

Responsiveness to changes

Adaptability starts with determining what the changes are (or might be) and responding to them. This starts right at the outset in the earliest activities of the master test plan: when determining and taking stock of the assignment, obtaining insight into the environment in which a test is executed, and establishing possible changes – taken together, all of these play a major part.

This is precisely where the basis is created for the further elaboration and implementation of the test. Which test levels, test types, phases, and tools are used and how? But it is not limited to these activities. The test strategy and associated plan are defined in close consultation with the client. If the test strategy and derived estimate and plan are not acceptable to the client, the plan is altered.

This emphasis gives the client control of the test process, enabling him to manage on the basis of the balance between risk and result, on the one hand, and time and cost, on the other.

Reuse of products and processes

Being able to use existing products and processes quickly is a requirement for adaptability. SOA consists of services, and specific test products are created for each of these services. Maybe one of these products can be used for testing another service (after a slight change)? For instance, some output created by a service during a test can be used as input for the test of another service. This can also be the case for a test harness that is developed for a specific service. After some modification it may be used at some other place in the SOA. A last example is the regression test. This can be created on the basis of the existing test scripts and test harnesses. It is therefore important to have continuous insight into what kind of test products are being created for which service.

Besides this reusing of products between services, it is also advisable to reuse the products of a test for a specific service. When the test is done, you should not throw everything away but preserve it for future use. For instance, when something needs to be changed in the service due to changing requirements, it may be convenient that previously created test scripts can be reused for the test. In addition, it is therefore necessary to set up the test so that products and processes are well preserved for further use and reuse.

Learn from experience

It is important to learn from and apply what has already been used. Therefore, it is of critical importance to evaluate the test process. Another important tool is the use of metrics. For the test process, metrics on the quality of the services and the progress and quality of the test process are extremely important. They are used to manage the test process, justify test recommendations, and compare systems or test processes. Metrics are also important to improve the test process by assessing the consequences of introducing certain test process improvement measures.

Try before use

When testing SOA, there must be scope in the plan to try something on a trial basis before it is actually used. The main tools here are activities related to doing an intake. An intake is an activity in which, on the basis of a checklist, it is determined whether the subject meets the previously set requirements regarding quality. For instance, doing an intake of the test basis (the information that defines the required behaviour of a service) enables you to check if the test basis has sufficient quality for use. Before starting with the preparation of the test and the creation of test scripts, you have to investigate the quality of this information. Often several suppliers of services are involved, so the quality of this information may be different each time. This can also be the case with the quality of a service.

Before a full-blown test of a specific service can start, it is advisable to do some sort of pre-test. The purpose of the pre-test is to evaluate whether or not the test object is of sufficient quality to proceed with further testing. The pre-test is carried out by executing specific test scripts that are created for this purpose. In real-life practice, a service is often wrongly delivered or wrongly installed in the first few days of testing, thus delaying the start of the test execution. This is not only a waste of time, it also demotivates the test team.

10.7 **Summary**

Before an organization starts using SOA, it has to ask itself which risks are being taken and which measures have been taken to mitigate those risks. To avoid obtaining answers to such crucial questions only during the operational phase of the SOA, a good, reliable testing process is required in advance of going operational. A testing process in a SOA world is different from 'traditional' software development, and this can be summarized in four statements:

1. Who owns, who pays?
2. When to test which service?
3. How to test a service?
4. A lot of services, a lot of testing

To set up testing so that it covers the important risks for a SOA implementation, the business-driven test management (BDTM) approach is used. This is based on the fact that if you spend money on SOA you will want to know what you are getting in return. The theory of IT Governance controls SOA projects on the basis of four aspects: *result, risk, time,* and *cost*. When testing SOA, this economic justification of IT plays an important role and it must be translated into the activity of testing. BDTM ensures the generation of the relationship between these aspects.

BDTM starts from the principle that the selected test approach must enable the client to control the test process and (help) determine the test approach. This gives the testing a business-like and rational character. The required information to make this possible is delivered from the test process.

A fitting test environment is required for the dynamic testing of SOA. The set-up and composition of a test environment depends on the aim of the test. With SOA, an organization can use an increasing number of different types of hardware and software. The layout of these test environments is a challenge, which, whatever the case, the testers must face. To organize this properly, the various stakeholders have to agree in advance on the finalization of the master test plan. A recommendation is to create the role of 'chain coordinator' in the test organization.

SOA can help organizations to change, although it is often thought that testing and continuous change are enemies. As a tester you need the capability to adapt to changing situations and needs. Besides being able to respond to the changing environment, it is also important to be able to leverage changes for the benefit of testing. Being adaptive as a tester can be summarized in four properties of adaptability:

• Responsiveness to changes.
• Reuse of products and processes.
• Learn from experience.
• Try before use.

11 Ten great things to say to get fired

Service Oriented Architecture offers great opportunities to improve the way in which business and IT work together. However, there are many pitfalls to be avoided along the road toward this promising future. Most of these pitfalls are related to the difficulty of adopting a new way of thinking about business and IT.

In this chapter we present ten of the most frequently heard ideas that may sound like 'a good idea' at some time along the way, but are actually 'great ways to get you fired'. We shall present an overview of these ideas, as well as the impact they might have, and some alternative choices that should be made.

Ten things to say to get you fired:
1. Let's not tell the business
2. Trust me: SOA is small, SOA is easy
3. We don't need process orientation
4. We WILL build a tower of Babel
5. Let's ask our new junior Enterprise Architect
6. Let's change the standards
7. With SOA we'll start aiming at moving targets
8. SOA? Just let a thousand flowers bloom
9. Let's do SO without A
10. We'll migrate everything to SOA

11.1 'Let's not tell the business'

SOA is all about business *and* IT. Yet still there are people in IT who think it is better to start with SOA without involving the business. Or worse: they plan to completely reimplement their IT using SOA principles without telling the business.

Why would this seem to make sense? For one, experience teaches us that it is often difficult to talk to the business about IT issues. Over the years, IT has lost a lot of credit with the business, and is now under pressure to 'just deliver'. Most discussions between business and IT are about projects, deadlines, and whether or not IT can be made more efficient. So it seems logical for an IT manager to use SOA as a shiny new way of improving the efficiency of IT, and not bother business with it.

There are at least two things that will go wrong with this kind of thinking: strategy and funding.

IT strategy
If IT really wishes to optimize itself, it must know what to expect. It ought to know which new initiatives will be started by the business, which new product will be developed, what will happen with business partners, suppliers, business processes etc. It's no use optimizing a system that will be obsolete within two years as a result of changing market circumstances. IT will surely have some idea of the general trends, but that does not have the same value as a genuine IT strategy that is formulated and owned by IT and business. IT needs a clear yardstick, defined by the business, by which to measure good and bad. With each decision it must be able to assess which option is better, which option is worse. (In a sense, IT and business are conjoined 'for better or for worse'.)

The underlying problem with this not-so-good idea of not telling the business is that there is not enough dialogue between business and IT to start with. It should be impossible for IT to undertake an architecture transformation without involving the business.

Funding
Another reason why it should be impossible to implement such important changes within IT without involving the business is that it is the business that ultimately pays for it. When thinking about reuse, tooling or new infrastructure (like an enterprise service bus), a new way of calculating cost must be implemented. Business wants to know what it is paying for, and especially what it will receive in return. But the project-based funding of IT to which we have grown accustomed will have to change. These changes are not limited to the IT level, they go beyond that. A business unit in an organization generally doesn't want to depend on any other business unit for its projects. SOA, however, will create shared infrastructure, shared services, and even shared sub processes that will be used by many different business units, projects, or processes. That is the whole point of implementing SOA. But if there is no policy in place to support this commonality, the organizational silos will remain in

place and will force IT to replicate those silos in the architecture. In this type of situation, reuse will remain an illusion.

At the start

The stubborn IT manager might reject the idea of involving the business right from the start, saying something like 'we first must build our own understanding of SOA within IT before we are able to address the demand from the business'. No matter how logical this may sound, it is wrong. Of course, IT has to learn a lot when adopting SOA. But the business side of the organization has to learn at least as much, and therefore should start on its own learning curve as early as possible. The same goes for statements like 'but we first have to implement some new this or that', or 'we must first clean up some old mess'. It is undeniable that SOA requires a lot of 'cleaning up' but this is not limited to IT. Business has to start rethinking its business processes and prepare for things to come. The way to get the most out of SOA is to develop jointly, and to close the gap between business and IT by entering and going through the learning curve together.

Talking to the business

So, should business get to know all about SOA? Should it be involved in all the steps along the way? Yes! But: on a business level. Strategic dialogue should be about business strategy, setting priorities, and making decisions from a business perspective. Business should not be bothered by acronyms or technical explanations. Within the dialogue a realistic, hype-free vision of SOA can be developed that determines the real business value of SOA. Business can state 'what' it wants in a crystal-clear manner. IT can reclaim its role by taking responsibility for 'how' this is to be accomplished. (As a consequence business can no longer waltz in saying 'we're buying this new IT system', it can only state which processes it wants supported and ought to allow IT to decide on the best way to do this.) But the main goal is to create an open dialogue from equal positions. IT can inspire business by spotting new business opportunities that may arise from new developments in the IT world. And business can inspire IT by sharing what other businesses are accomplishing with their IT.

> **Exceptions to the rule**
>
> It hardly ever happens, but in the very rare case when an organization has one homogeneous IT environment (all mainframe or all SAP for example), there is hardly any need for SOA. There are usually no integration issues, there is a lot of insight into the system, and the response to business changes will be prompt and reliable. In this case (only), it is a perfectly defendable strategy to simply follow suit with the vendors' upgrades. Business will notice little of any 'upgrade' to SOA in this kind of situation. Nevertheless: strategic dialogue is required to make sure future demand can be met while following the vendors' lead.

11.2 'Trust me: SOA is small, SOA is easy'

While the basic concepts of SOA are easy, putting them into practice is not. A lot of SOA initiatives fail because they were sold as quick fixes that would deliver significant results. It's important to realize that SOA in itself will not solve the hard problems of integration, legacy, and IT strategy. SOA *will* provide a framework with best practices that can be used to determine and create your solution.

Sin or ignorance?

Ignoring the complexity of SOA will be costly. Regardless of how simple the concepts of SOA may be, it has a wide impact and the hard questions remain just as hard. Underestimating the impact or complexity will cause investments in IT projects to fail, and even more goodwill to be lost between business and IT. If SOA sounds too good to be true, it will be just that: too good to be true. Selling SOA as a quick fix will delay real improvement for years. There are quite a few examples of IT organizations starting SOA projects that were ultimately stopped by the business as a consequence of failing to show any relevant result for the business. Lots of time and effort have been wasted in building the perfect architecture that nobody asked for.

Evolution, not revolution

A maturity model, like the one discussed in this book, gives a good overview of the impact of SOA, of which steps should be taken first, and of which steps come later. It should be used as a guide to managing expectations: which business benefits will be realized when, and in which order. SOA can be implemented like an evolution: small steps, each of which has (some) business value.

11.3 'We don't need process orientation'

There are many ways to look at an organization. Usually there's a product view in which the specific products or services offered are central to the way of thinking. Opposite to that is the process view, in which not the products themselves matter most, but the processes that partners or customers use to do things: to request a new policy, to change an address, or to ask a question.

With SOA, we look at the core services an organization provides. These services are related to products as much as process. But above all, the services relate to the (core) capabilities an organization possesses: the things an organization can do. To find out what its capabilities are, there needs to be insight into the workings of the organization. In this way it's like designing a traditional IT system: only when the processes to be supported are known can a design for the system be made to fit day-to-day business.

Since Service Oriented Architecture is much more valuable when applied throughout an organization, there needs to be insight into processes that run through the entire organization: abandoning boundaries within the company, or even looking beyond the boundaries between the organization and the outside world. Currently, the most practical way of looking at an organization across boundaries is to take the process-oriented view: look from outside inward, to find the processes that make up the organization.

Without this process view, your SOA will most probably become a siloed architecture that may fit current products, but will not provide the desired agility.

To summarize, SOA tries to automate an organization along the lines of how the processes really work and not along the lines of how it's structured. This requires a process-oriented approach.

11.4 'We WILL build a tower of Babel'

Integration is hard because it isn't an IT-only issue. Multiple systems connect, technology is used to transport data and perhaps also to transform some data, so that there's a fit between the sending and receiving systems. Many more technical issues may have to be solved, such as security, reliability, performance, etc. But there's one more important condition that has to be met in order to connect systems: it must make sense to connect them in the first place. That is: the connection must be possible on a conceptual level. A number representing a product in one system must be transformable to a product in another system, and accounting data from one end must be integratable with data from the other end. Or, on a business level: something like 'occupancy' for airplanes has to mean the same thing to different departments: does that include staff? Does that include passengers rebooked from another flight? Does it include passengers who paid but didn't actually fly? Depending on which department you ask, you might get a different answer: accounting may see things different from the planning department, etc. For their underlying systems to be integratable, there must be a business agreement on how to interpret data. And not only an agreement on data, there must also be agreement on processes, expected quality, ownership, etc. The wisdom from the biblical story about the tower of Babel is proven again: if everybody speaks a different language, cooperation towards a common goal becomes very complicated, if not impossible.

What's the sin?

Leaving integration to IT will have them make decisions that really can only be taken on a business level. This will result in systems that do not reflect the way real business works.

This can also occur on a different scale with the so-called 'bottom-up' definition of services: IT looking to salvage reusable bits of code from existing systems and renaming them 'services'. This might work, and it might accidentally result in usable systems, but there is no *guarantee* that the services will provide business value.

So, as we mentioned before, in order to steer the well-intended initiatives away from IT, business must take its responsibility in integration and SOA. Business must take the lead in integration, and be actively involved in defining processes, dictionaries, service levels, and many other integration issues. Often this is worked out in governance structures and setting up good architecture processes. Business behaving like 'absentee landlords' simply is unacceptable

11.5 'Let's ask our new Junior Enterprise Architects'

New developments provide new career opportunities for young, bright minds who know everything about these new developments. SOA is no different. People who recently started in IT, and who accept SOA as the logical way of doing IT, will prove to be of great value when implementing SOA.

Yet, there's a risk as well: it's called reinventing the wheel. With SOA, we see that a lot of young bright stars have a background in technology. They started programming web services, using cool new tools to generate all sorts of solutions. Now they have grown into advising the business on how to use SOA. But they lack experience in business processes, governance, or organizational change.

As we have seen, SOA has a wide impact on organizations. Most of the impact is not technological but organizational: changing the way processes work, changing the way governance is arranged, etc. This is where experience must complement intelligence and knowledge of the latest technological developments. Really determining value, seeing what's realistic and what's not, requires practical experience.

Junior Enterprise Architects tend to discover for themselves how architecture works, how governance should be done, how a useful IT strategy ought to be chosen, etc. Of course we think that books can help, but experience in your organization is of much greater value. Service Oriented Architecture is a very powerful tool, but it requires both theoretical and practical understanding of what it really is and how it is best applied. If one of the two is absent, you should not use it, because it will backfire. The first step toward using SOA is learning what it really is, and how to use it. Initiatives in which organizations start exchanging experiences within an industry have proven valuable in building practical knowledge of how to apply it best.

A splendid way to ensure that experience and fresh knowledge get together is to start up a SOA Competence Center (or SOA Center of Excellence) in which the leading SOA architects are represented. Logically this Competence Center will receive the explicit mandate to build the knowledge while keeping SOA initiatives on track.

11.6 'Let's change the standards'

One of the easy concepts of Service Oriented Architecture involves using standards. In this sense, 'standards' are the international, big standards, but also the standards used within your company. Once an agreement is made on how to solve a certain issue, it becomes a standard.

If we really want to cut maintenance costs, these standards have to be used as intended, without changes or deviations. If somewhere one programmer gets a chance of cutting a corner by slightly 'enhancing' a standard, you lose the benefits of easier maintenance and lower costs. If a new system that relies on the 'official' standard is to be implemented, and it cannot use the slightly 'enhanced' standard, we're back at square one: manual changes to make sure everything works.

To make this work, there must be discipline, governance, and control. But what is needed above all: everybody must share the vision of why it's so important to adhere to standards as agreed upon. This also holds true for the business. Once a standard has been chosen it cannot be set aside because some new tool has to be implemented quickly. Long-term objectives like flexibility, consistency and reuse should not be sacrificed for short-term goals or priorities. Standards only work if everybody adheres to them.

11.7 'With SOA, we'll start aiming at moving targets'

Agility is the desired goal. It may seem logical to assume that, with SOA, all the IT will be constantly changing to keep in line with business. Just as scope creep in any project will make it unmanageable, agile *everything* will not deliver on the promises of SOA. Agility has to be created exactly at the 'hotspots' of change. The real secret of successful SOA is to make the distinction between things that will change and things that will not.

This will be done from an IT perspective, looking at technical components that will last for some time and can be configured to respond to changing business demand. It will be done from a business perspective by finding those processes and requirements that are more durable than most others. This search for the changing and non-changing aspects of IT or business is really the 'emerging architecture': finding and defining the structures that will last longer than the day-to-day changes.

Business architecture is all about finding the core capabilities and processes: what does your company really do, now and in the future? What are the 'eternal' truths we can count on? And this is where we return to the most important message: this can only be accomplished by having a strategic dialogue between business and IT. Through this dialogue, business (architects) will learn to think about future business developments and innovation and make the translation into requirements for present day IT.

11.8 'Just let a thousand flowers bloom'

It may seem like a good idea to let projects build and deploy services as much as they like, letting each project solve its own problems. It may seem clever to decide on possible duplicate services later. Or solve problems when they arise, in the case of services that don't integrate well to serve a business purpose.

Here we should learn from the past. With the emergence of the internet, there was a sudden abundance of new solutions that were easy to build, easy to deploy, sprouting up all over. And we're still paying the maintenance cost of all these semi-redundant systems, each of which has its own database, server, or tooling. There is a serious risk that this will happen again with services: within a few years there may be more services within your organization than can reasonably be maintained by any IT staff. One of the reasons is that it's just *too* easy to create new services.

An impressive example of how fast services can germinate is that of an insurance company which let a few projects start with little or no guidance or control. After just a few months, between six and ten services had been implemented to provide the same customer data: each service with its own slight deviation.

Lesson from the past: there is no 'later'
If you want to have something done properly, you should start right from the beginning. It's very hard to correct things from the past once they are there. Instead of thinking 'we can improve our services portfolio at a later stage', it should be 'we have to manage our services portfolio right from the start'.

What to do?

There are a few things that can be done to ensure the manageability of your services portfolio. For one: generate an architecture process to talk about and implement architecture within projects. Only when there's a shared vision on the enterprises architecture will enterprise architecture really develop. On a more practical note, make sure that the right tooling is used to manage services right from the outset. Directory tooling allows for the listing of existing and future services, including service levels, ownership, versioning, etc.

Survival of the fittest

With SOA, the set of services that IT provides must closely fit the demand from the business. A constantly changing business also means the portfolio of services is under continuous scrutiny: services will disappear, services will be modified, new services will be made available, services will be reconfigured. In the end, only those services that best fit the demand of the business and for which there is a real business case will survive.

11.9 'Let's do SO without A'

There is overwhelming evidence that Services or 'Service Orientation' without sound architecture does not work. At the same time, most press and internet coverage is about tooling, technology or vendors of SOA-related software. Service Oriented Architecture is not a tool or a product that comes in a box: Service Oriented Architecture really is an Architecture.

There needs to be structure, control, and coherence. Services need to be aligned with business. Projects need to think about inter-project concerns. IT needs to find and define the non-changing and changing parts of IT. You really need Architecture to make SOA work. Without architecture, the risk that services pose is bigger than the opportunity they offer.

And for architecture to work, it will be 'just enough, just in time' and solidly anchored in the day-to-day processes of IT. Architecture needs processes just as much as it needs models and abstractions. And architecture does not arise bottom-up: it's a top-down decision to implement and sponsor architecture within business and IT.

11.10 'Let's migrate everything to SOA!'

When learning about SOA, it will seem like a good model that can be used to structure IT. So migration or upgrading all existing IT to Service Oriented Architecture might appear an attractive proposition. Let's face it, who would not like to get rid of all the old stuff? But, we don't like a big bang: there's too much risk. We don't even really like 'big': it's usually too expensive to make any business sense. So how does SOA fit in?

SOA can be implemented in a gradual way: applying more and more principles to more and more parts of IT. As shown in the maturity model, different aspects can be improved at different times. So it seems that SOA doesn't require a 'bang' to be implemented.

It's good to have this vision of the ideal world in which everything is SOA. It can serve as a guide in showing what could be reached within your company. Yet at the same time: architectural principles should be applied 'just enough, just in time'. Real business-driven IT also requires investments to be closely related to business goals and risks. No business case can be found that justifies replacing all IT systems with service-enabling ones, just as there is no benefit in retrofitting two systems that only communicate with one another, and there is no business case that can support upgrading the existing email system with a 'service oriented' one.

As holds true for all models: only your *specific* goals determine how much of the model you should implement. You have to find your specific SOA target level. How much SOA you need, where you need it, and what you can expect from it greatly depends on your business.

A sin or simply enthusiasm?
How serious is this sin of wanting to migrate everything to SOA? It should be regarded as a cardinal sin because it goes against the primary objective of SOA: to make IT simpler. SOA is popular because of its promise to turn IT into the manageable, efficient, effective support for business it always should have been. We only extensively test the things that pose a business risk, we only optimize the things that provide business optimization, we only change because it improves the way business can be done. Saying that *all* IT must be changed to SOA implies that SOA becomes a goal in itself, thus missing the point completely.

A side note

While generally there will be no business case for large scale all-or-nothing migrations to SOA, there may be rare (that means: not in your company) exceptions to this rule: in some cases external providers might offer services that match internal processes so closely that enough change is taking place to build momentum. It becomes feasible to finally break from historically grown legacy systems and start anew. Especially in industries where commoditization is taking place at a high speed, service providers will be eager to fill gaps that appear in this new commoditized market. And in some cases the internal mess is big enough to warrant a radical step forward: rebuild it all from scratch.

How much, when, how?

In the maturity model presented in this book, you will find a valuable tool for seeking out the steps that need to be taken, and the order of sequence for moving up the SOA ladder. In addition to that, you will need to develop a vision of SOA and how it can help in your specific situation: tie in the business goals, IT problems and existing IT operation, and relate them to SOA benefits. From then on, you can build your own roadmap to SOA.

12 The journey continues

So where have we been and where can we go from here? In this book we have shown how you can use Service Oriented Architecture for profit. We have described the benefits you can expect, such as increased agility and lower maintenance costs. We have talked about how SOA can address long-running issues in business and IT, such as solving integration issues and reusing existing legacy.

As we have seen, the concepts behind SOA are simple and based on experience with IT in the past 30 years. Simple concepts like componentization, doing things for a business reason, and trying to reuse components wherever possible make up this architecture. Starting to use this architecture is a transformation that needs careful planning and governance. And with SOA increasing the agility in IT, governance and architecture are key factors to keep business and IT aligned and prevent SOA initiatives from running wild.

An IT environment based on SOA enables new ways of doing business, and service oriented principles can be applied to the business processes themselves. To find the business services that make up your business, and to look at your business at the right level of abstraction, you need to understand your business (that's easy) and find a way of modeling it. We have demonstrated how to drill down using several views that result in a set of future-proof capabilities and services that define the essence of your business.

The introduction of SOA has direct consequences for the people and the roles they fulfil in your organization. An important role is defined for the enterprise architect, who will personally help close the gap that usually exists between business and IT. The enterprise architect will help guide the organization along the transformation to SOA. Besides addressing the people aspect, we have also talked about how SOA will impact the organization itself. We have introduced a model called the Human Services Bus that can be used to reach maximum agility with SOA. We have also defined which organizational elements will need to be in place to enable the necessary governance.

To make things practical, you can start by defining your business vision and strategy, and then use a maturity model to build your organization-specific roadmap to SOA. The maturity model will point out the aspects in your organization that need to be improved in order to reach the level of SOA adoption that is necessary to execute your business strategy. Since building your SOA is largely done in 'ordinary' business-driven projects, extra attention is devoted to defining possible entry points that outline suitable SOA projects. We also explore how a mature testing process can serve as a guide to avoiding risks when implementing SOA.

So here we are, at a crossroads in the future history of IT. A new way of looking at IT has been introduced, and there's value to be found in using it. Using it isn't exactly simple, but it is manageable and gradual. It looks like a good road to follow. But what's further up the road?

12.1 Destinations ahead

When Service Oriented Architecture becomes the leading architecture model, and companies free themselves of their legacy and inflexible IT, new opportunities will arise and start changing the business world. Similar to the way internet gradually but radically changed customer interactions, SOA will change business interaction with partners, suppliers, and customers. It will change the way we use IT and the way we do business. We shall give you a glimpse of a possible future with SOA. At best, it will be many years from now, if we ever get there at all.

Flexibility changes business

Companies that are no longer restrained by slow changing IT will move quicker, and will be able to respond better to changing circumstances. New business models will arise, like the Human Services Bus model, where organizational units become loosely coupled and can start providing their services across organizational boundaries. Your secretary might start doing work for other companies, just because there's a business case for her to do so. Intermediaries, who used to just sell your services, will compose a custom set of services that will best fit the demand from any individual customer.

Focus on the core

The distinction between 'infrastructural' IT and 'innovative' IT will become clearer, giving organizations the freedom to focus on their core activities and invest in the important parts of their business. No longer will more than half of all the money go to keeping the company running. Most of the money can then be invested in value creation and innovation. This will be extra valuable in a world where businesses are in need of constant increase of effectiveness and efficiency to address large and expensive issues like globalization, ageing, and the threat of climate change.

The new world of the internet

By providing services using SOA, companies will be suitably equipped to enter the new marketplace: the global internet market in which the world is flat and service providers from all over the world compete for customers. The internet will evolve from a network of information into a network of services. Just as you can now look up the weather, you will then be able to look up any business function you need: who will do my HR for this price? Who will fabricate this product for me within this timeframe?

A long tail and a wide nose

With the new business models, making a modification in a business process or adding new capabilities doesn't disturb the entire organization. It makes it easier to innovate. If it becomes easy enough, it will even be possible to innovate by using trial and error: define a wide scope of new products or services and just see which of these are an immediate hit, or investigate how some of them should be modified to find the greatest markets.

With the worldwide market on the internet already giving us a long tail, by providing demand and a delivery model for niche products and services, easy innovation also gives us a wide nose. This wide nose is the widening scope of innovation to increase the chances of sniffing out the next great thing, or next niche. In turn, trial and error innovation will fit perfectly into Web 2.0 trends, where social networks and actions of many individuals directly help shape innovation. Crowd-sourcing your innovation, and combining it with the ability to easily innovate your assortment will give you the keys to the market. Service oriented offerings that are open to combination and personalization will make this possible.

New generations

New generations, the digital natives, will enter this arena, taking up the solutions that are there and bringing them to a new level. They will make the technology meet their expectations of how IT should work: ubiquitous, always on, invisible, and totally reliable. Privacy is less of an issue, they will expect IT solutions to follow their lead effortlessly in whatever they do: adapt to individual processes and personal preferences. Their movements on the internet and in social, virtual worlds are an important part of their identity. IT helps them express themselves and be productive. There will be a crossover between work and play, where IT is never a restriction but always enabling. Service Oriented Architecture will provide the services they'll use to build their IT world.

The next step in the evolution of new media will embed technology into everyday life to an ever greater extent, and let it fade into the background by blending with all sorts of 'old' media like TV, phones, and even print. Interfacing with the digital world will blend in with interfacing with the world we know.

IT in its final role
A large part of IT will come to rest as the infrastructure that it should be: common services taking care of common things. Storing customer data, handling payments, shipping goods will no longer be organization or unit-specific. They will be infrastructure, ready to use when needed, optimized for low cost and high efficiency. Starting with some shared high-level models or shared data definitions, the common elements will be increasingly readily available as time goes on. The large software vendors are embracing more open business models to allow the mixing of technologies. Description-based IT will become feasible, building IT solutions without programming or configuration, using only meta descriptions of the organization such as process descriptions, a capability map, and a services map.

A small but essential part of IT will still enable business innovation. New advances in IT will provide companies with a competitive edge, although it may be for just a short period of time. They will try to follow the leading edge technologies and find business value in them by means of trial and error.

12.2   But only if...

The journey to this potential future SOA world will not be easy. Continuously balancing short-term gain and long-term improvement still requires serious management attention. The sheer complexity of combined new developments might be overwhelming. A clear innovation process is essential in order to generate a strategy to deal with these developments. Developing a mature IT organization while handling things like day-to-day Human Resource challenges will not be a short-term project. Developing a shared long-term vision, and keeping it up to date, will gradually improve all interconnected aspects of business and IT.

In this book we have talked about the most important conditions for guiding your company toward successful SOA. Your organization can expect great benefits from SOA, but only if:
- You have *Structured Governance* to keep the organization in line with changing circumstances and keep IT in line with a changing business.
- You use *Sound Architecture* to make governance actionable and link it to IT developments.
- You develop a *Broad vision of* SOA to make sure SOA is not approached as a technological development, or presented as a 'quick fix' solution for important problems in the current IT organization.

12.3 Call to action

Whatever the future may hold: it will be here faster than you can imagine. The speed of change is continuously increasing, intensifying the urgency to get rid of restricting IT structures.

If you want your company to be ready for this new world, start on the journey toward SOA now. Take a look at your current maturity; build a business vision and a SOA strategy to make sure your company will also be able to play a significant role in a SOA world.

Get to work, start small but don't try to cut corners: grow in equilibrium by addressing all the different aspects that are needed for mature cooperation between business and IT.

13 Appendix: SOA Maturity Model

13.1 Introduction

The SOA Maturity Model was introduced in Chapter 8. This instrument enables any organization wanting to prepare for SOA to devote the right amount of attention to the right area at the right time. The SOA Maturity Model helps you to recognize the appropriate steps for improvement in the areas of Process, Technology, and People, which have priority at any given time.

First of all, to identify the appropriate improvement steps, it is necessary to assess SOA readiness in terms of the Maturity Model's 20 key areas. This Appendix will help you perform this assessment. This Appendix identifies checkpoints for each level of each key area to determine whether or not an organization has attained the level in question.

To appreciate the structure of this Appendix, it is helpful to refer to the SOA Maturity Model.

In the Maturity Model, the columns represent stages on the pathway of increasing maturity. The rows contain the 20 key areas. The letters in the model indicate the level of maturity at each stage. The step-by-step improvement progresses from left to right in the model.

Observe the following rules in applying the Maturity Model:
- An organization attains a level when all the checkpoints at that level and all preceding levels have been satisfied.
- An organization achieves a stage of maturity when all the levels at that stage and at all previous stages have been attained.

Individual sections devoted to each of the key areas in the SOA Maturity Model are presented in the order that the areas are listed in the model, beginning with *Commitment and Motivation*. The levels (A, B, C, and D) in each of the areas will be discussed. Checkpoints are provided for each level. These can be used to establish where you are in terms of your organization's position, and how you might improve it.

	Key area	Stage 0	1	2	3	4	5	6	7	8	9	10	11	12	13
1	Commitment and motivation		A				B				C				
2	Relationships with projects			A			B	C					D		
3	Roles and responsibility			A			B		C						
4	Development of architecture			A				B		C					
5	Use of architecture				A				B		C				
6	Architectural tools (methodology and software)					A				B			C		
7	Quality Management						A			B		C			D
8	Service portfolio management					A			B		C				D
9	Vision of architecture		A		B		C							D	
10	Alignment with business			A			B		C			D			
11	Budgeting and planning			A				B		C			D		
12	Technology and standards		A				B					C	D		
13	Componentization and Reuse			A				B				C			D
14	Business processes implementation in the Information System				A					B		C			D
15	Information System (infrastructure and applications) flexibility			A	B							C			D
16	Information Security		A			B			C			D			
17	SOA skills in IT			A				B			C				
18	SOA skills in Business			A				B			C				
19	SOA mindset and knowledge among IT People		A				B			C					
20	SOA mindset and knowledge among Business People		A				B			C					

Figure 13.1 SOA Maturity Model

13.2 Commitment and motivation

A: Budget and time available for SOA initiatives

A budget and time are made available for a limited number of SOA initiatives. These initiatives ought to demonstrate that SOA has added value for the organization. SOA has not yet been accepted as the future preferred architectural direction for the organization.

Checkpoints:
- Is there a budget available for SOA initiatives?
- Is there time available for SOA initiatives?
- Is SOA regarded by business and IT management as an important development?

B: SOA approach is sponsored by the management of the organization

SOA is now generally accepted as the preferred architectural style for business and IT, and the top management of the organization propagates this choice.

Checkpoints:
- Is SOA actively promoted by the business and IT management?
- In the implementation of new functionality, is SOA the standard choice as the preferred architectural style?

C: SOA approach is integrated in the organization processes

The choice for SOA is now completely integrated in all processes of the organization. There is a broad support base for the idea that SOA has strategic value for the organization and that continuous attention is justified.

Checkpoints:
- Has old functionality been proactively replaced by new functionality based on SOA?
- Is SOA a vital item among the organization staff?
- Has a chapter on SOA been included in the project plans as a standard item?
- Does the management deliberately steer projects in such a way that they comply with SOA-based enterprise architecture?
- Is SOA included in the strategic plan of the organization?

13.3 Relationships with projects

A: Architecture to project communication

Architects bring the SOA-based architecture to the project, but there is still little interaction between the architect and the project and there is no feedback from the project to the architect so that the things learned during the project can be processed in the architecture.

Checkpoints:
- Do projects take account of the SOA-based enterprise architecture?
- At the outset, are projects informed of the SOA-based enterprise architecture?

B: Architectural process takes project feedback into account

The architectural process between the architecture and the projects has been regulated to the extent that architects can gather feedback from the projects and adapt the SOA architecture if necessary.

Checkpoints:
- Is the SOA-based enterprise architecture adjusted on the basis of experience obtained with it in various projects?
- Does compliance with SOA-based enterprise architecture have a place in the standard development process?

C: Architects, business and IT jointly build the project architecture

The creation of the Project Start Architecture is a joint process in which architects and their most important stakeholders are involved.

Checkpoints:
- Do the architects help the developers to orient the SOA-based enterprise architecture to their specific situation?
- Can developers propose modifications to the SOA-based enterprise architecture?
- Is the SOA-based project architecture the result of cooperation between the architects and the developers?

D: Continuous dialogue between architects, business and IT

There is a continuous dialogue in which architects and their most important stakeholders mutually align the reference architecture, Project Start Architecture, and their experiences with these, and subsequently adapt products and projects where necessary.

Checkpoints:
- Is there a standard process by means of which the interaction between architects and projects occurs?
- Is there a standard process that specifies the way in which modifications to project deliverables should be processed in architecture deliverables?
- Is there standard consultation between architects and developers on how mutual cooperation can be improved?

13.4 Roles and responsibilities

A: IT department in charge of architecture and process
The IT department is responsible for the SOA-based architecture and the process of implementing SOA. No clear roles and definitions have been defined for the business.

Checkpoints:
- Is it clear why the organization has opted for SOA as the preferred architectural style?
- Has the responsibility for the SOA-based enterprise architecture been embedded in the organization?
- Has the responsibility for the identification, specification, building and phasing out of services (service life cycle) been embedded in the organization?
- Have the roles and responsibilities for the implementation of SOA been embedded in the organization?

B: IT and business collaborate in architectural process
IT and business now collaborate in an architectural process, and on both sides the roles and responsibilities for the implementation of SOA have been defined.

Checkpoints:
- Has ownership of a service been embedded in the business?
- Has ownership of the service portfolio been embedded in the business?
- Have the roles and responsibilities for the implementation of SOA been embedded in the business and IT?

C: Responsibility of process ownership is transversal
The responsibility for end-to-end business processes has been embedded and extends trouble free through all business-unit departments.

Checkpoints:
- Has the end-to-end responsibility for business processes been embedded in the organization?
- Has the responsibility for the reuse of services been embedded in the business?
- In the implementation of SOA, does the end-to-end business process objective carry more weight than the business unit or department objective?

13.5 Development of architecture

A: Architecture undertaken in projects
The formulation of SOA-based architecture deliverables takes place in connection with a concrete project, such as Project Start Architecture.

Checkpoints:
- Have all the stakeholders been informed that the organization has opted for SOA as the preferred architectural style?
- Has a SOA-oriented architectural description been formulated for each project?
- If project architecture or Project Start Architecture are already standard in use, is specific attention being devoted to SOA?

B: Architecture as a transversal process
Setting up SOA-based architecture now takes place across the projects and the departments, as reference architecture for example.

Checkpoints:
- Are there general SOA principles and models within the organization that apply to all the projects?
- Is there enterprise architecture within the organization in which specific attention is devoted to SOA?
- Is there some form of release management for the enterprise architecture?

C: Architecture as a facilitation process

The generation of SOA-based architecture takes place as a component of an architectural process in which people are aware that the only goal of architecture is to support the changes that are needed to realize the business objectives. With every form of architecture that is set up, it is clear right from the outset what the aim and function of the architecture are.

Checkpoints:
- Are SOA principles and models an inextricable component of the enterprise architecture of the organization?
- Have all the stakeholders accepted the organization's choice for SOA as the preferred architectural style?
- In the setting up of the enterprise architecture, has it been established who is going to act upon the outcome?

13.6 Use of architecture

A: Architecture used informatively

The SOA-based architecture provides a clear picture of where the organization wishes to go with SOA, and inspires people to pursue this aim. In addition, this picture is propagated by the management. All the members of staff have access to the architecture.

Checkpoints:
- Is there an enterprise architecture that has been approved by management?
- Does the enterprise architecture give a clear picture of what the organization wants?
- Is clear why SOA was chosen as the preferred architectural style?
- Is the enterprise architecture accessible to all members of staff?

B: Architecture used to steer content

The SOA-based architecture is genuinely used to steer the options in the field of SOA in projects. Projects ought to comply with the architecture.

Checkpoints:
- Is the enterprise architecture used to guide the business and IT developments in advance?

- Does a particular project have a clear view of which part of the enterprise architecture it is concerned with?
- Does a project have a clear view of the extent to which it has to comply with the enterprise architecture?

C: Architecture integrated into the organization

The SOA-based architecture is an integral component of the steering of the organization. It is an important factor in the decision-making processes.

Checkpoints:
- Is enterprise architecture used in the decision-making processes of the organization?
- Is enterprise architecture used in the planning and control cycle of the organization?
- Is the vision on SOA based on the top management's vision of the organization?

13.7 Architectural tools (methodology and software)

A: Non-coordinated initiatives

Methods and tools are used in SOA initiatives but no particular attention is devoted to examining whether or not these methods and tools fit together well.

Checkpoints:
- Are methods and tools used to identify and model the services?
- Are methods and tools used to manage the service portfolio?
- Are methods and tools used to monitor the use of services?

B: Tooling streamlining and integration policy. A global architecture process is defined

Methods and tools are carefully chosen on the basis of a defined architectural process. Policy is formulated to ensure better mutual integration of the methods and tools.

Checkpoints:
- Do the methods and tools support the architecture process?
- Do the methods and tools support the development process?
- Do the methods and tools support the control process?

- Has the management of the methods and tools been explicitly embedded?
- Do the architects use the same tools?

C: Tooling is comprehensive and integrated. A global architecture process is formalized
A situation has been achieved in which the methods and tools are fully mutually integrated and fit perfectly into the architecture process.

Checkpoints:
- Can the complete life cycle of a service be managed with the aid of tools?
- Can the complete portfolio of services be managed with the aid of tools?
- Are the tools used integrated in any way?
- Do the architects, developers, and operational support use one single tool environment?

13.8 Quality management

A: Subsequent non-formal validation
The SOA-based architecture and ultimate project deliverables are validated retroactively, and an attempt is made to answer the question concerning whether the choices made and the project deliverables based on these are in line with the strategy and business goals of the organization. No norms have been defined in advance.

Checkpoints:
- Have attempts been undertaken to validate the SOA-based enterprise architecture in any way?
- Have attempts been undertaken to validate the designed services in any way?

B: A retroactive assessment is done on the basis of standardized indicators
The norms with which the SOA-based architecture and project deliverables must comply have been defined in advance. Validation must take place retroactively on the basis of these norms.

Checkpoints:
- Have quality norms been specified for the services?
- Have quality norms been specified for the enterprise architecture?

C: The IS architecture quality process is defined. There is continuous quality management.

A process has been laid out to guarantee the quality of the SOA-based architecture and project deliverables.

Checkpoints:
- Has a process been set up to guarantee the quality of the services?
- Is structural attention being devoted to the quality of the architecture process?
- Is there a quality programme for SOA?

D: The IS architecture quality process is integrated in the organization quality process

The guarantee of the quality of the architecture and the project deliverables is a part of an integral quality policy of the organization.

Checkpoints:
- Is the quality of enterprise architecture a part of the overarching quality policy of the organization?
- Is structural attention being devoted to the effect of implementing SOA in the organization?
- Is the relationship with processes in the organization (strategy forming processes, architecture processes, development processes, management processes) taken into account in quality considerations about SOA?

13.9 Service portfolio management

A: Life cycles of services follow those of applications delivering them

Business services are linked to an application and are adapted where necessary as the application is adapted.

Checkpoints:
- Is the management of a service linked to the application that provides this service?

- If necessary, is a service adapted when the application that provides this service is adapted?

B: Service Level Agreements

The management business services no longer primarily takes place on the basis of applications but on the basis of service contracts (service level agreements) in which the customer and supplier of the service make an agreement concerning the conditions under which the service is supplied.

Checkpoints:
- Is there a service contract for every service?
- Prior to a service being built, is a service contract containing the specifications and conditions under which the service is supplied formulated in advance?

C: Planned life cycle (including decommissioning)

Business services are now managed as a fully fledged portfolio. This means that decisions are taken on the entire life cycle of services related to the complete portfolio of services.

Checkpoints:
- Are the services of the organization managed as a portfolio?
- Is there a mechanism in which the price of a service is determined by its use?
- Are there clear agreements with regard to a service being reused?
- Are there clear agreements concerning what happens when a service is phased out?

D: Service usage funding (service market place)

A service marketplace has been laid out, where customers and suppliers of services negotiate with one another about the services. Making and rejecting services is the result of this negotiation process.

Checkpoints:
- Is it possible for a service supplier to phase out that service when negotiations with customers break down?
- Is the price of a service determined by the degree to which it is used?
- Can users and suppliers of services negotiate with one another on the conditions of delivery and the price?

13.10 Vision of architecture

A: Vision of 'as-is' architecture

The current state (as-is) architecture for business, information, and techno-logical architecture is known and specified. The shortcomings of the architecture are also clear.

Checkpoints:
- Is the current state (as-is) enterprise architecture described in terms of processes, services, applications, data, technical infrastructure, and the relationships between these?
- Are the bottlenecks in the current state enterprise architecture evident?

B: Vision of short-term evolutions

Besides the current state architecture, there is insight into the short-term SOA developments and the extent to which these influence the current state architecture. On this basis, a limited number of domain reference architectures are set up to steer short-term developments.

Checkpoints:
- Is it clear which components of the current state enterprise architecture are influenced by the choice for SOA.
- Does the enterprise architecture contain principles for identifying, designing, and building services?
- Are reference architectures (to-be or future state) available to those domains where SOA is being implemented?

C: Vision of long-term architecture

On the basis of the organization's strategy, a to-be enterprise architecture is set up to display the main contours of the changes in the field of business, information, and technological architecture. The organization now has at its disposal a long-term plan that reflects the organization's vision of the layout of business and IT.

Checkpoints:
- Is there an enterprise-wide reference architecture available in which the organization's vision of SOA is described?
- Does the organization have an enterprise architecture that has been accepted by top management?

D: Continuous alignment of vision with business goals, short and long-term

The organization has at its disposal a process by means of which architectural considerations enable the continuous alignment of strategy, business objectives and the current processes, organizational layout, provision of information, and technical infrastructure of an organization.

Checkpoints:

- Does the organization have at its disposal a process by means of which strategy is continuously aligned to current operations?
- Does the organization have at its disposal an enterprise architecture which clearly describes what the consequences of the organization's strategy for current operations and IT are?

13.11 Alignment of information systems with business

A: Applications and services are designed to meet business goals (business-driven)

Services and applications are designed by referring to the needs of the business and by establishing an explicit link with the business objectives.

Checkpoints:

- Are services and applications only designed when there is a clear business case for them?
- In the design of services and applications, is the primary starting point the notion that these must serve business objectives?
- Are the requirements of the business known prior to the services and applications being designed?

B: Applications and services are tested for compatibility with business goals

Services and applications are now tested retroactively with regard to compatibility with the needs and goals of the business.

Checkpoints:

- Is there retroactive validation (by means of testing, for example) of whether or not the built services and applications fulfil the specified requirements?
- Does the organization have at its disposal a formalized service testing process?

C: Architectural process supports the business

Services and applications are designed in an architectural process that is steered by the business objectives pursued by the organization. The services and applications that are designed are wholly determined by the business changes envisaged.

Checkpoints:
- Does the organization have at its disposal an architectural process that describes the steps by means of which the services and applications are designed?
- Does the organization have at its disposal an architectural process that starts with the strategy and business objectives of the organization?

D: Architectural process facilitates business transformations

Architectural consideration is an integral component of the organization. Architects and business representatives jointly participate in the strategic dialogue in which direction is given to the process of determining which services and applications are to be designed.

Checkpoints:
- Are business transformations only executed when architecture has been set up for this purpose?
- Does the business feel involved in the architectural process?
- Is the business a regular discussion partner in the set-up of the architecture?
- Are architects involved in the strategy forming processes?

13.12 Budgeting and planning

A: Need to formally justify a direct ROI for each SOA-impacted business project

Each project that has a SOA impact is tested on the basis of its yield (such as ROI = Return on Investment).

Checkpoints:
- Is each SOA project tested with regard to certain yield objectives?
- Is a budget drawn up for each SOA project?

B: SOA project specific
Each SOA project is preceded by the formulation of a planning schedule and the framing of a budget.

Checkpoints:
- Is a planning schedule formulated for each SOA project?
- Is the progress of a SOA project monitored?

C: Organization generic
There is a standard budgeting and planning method for SOA projects within the organization.

Checkpoints:
- Is there a standard budgeting and planning method for SOA projects?
- Are any deviations from the formulated budget and planning schedule accounted for and documented in the execution of SOA projects?

D: Continuous optimization of the budgeting and planning process
Budgeting and planning SOA projects can be professionalized by performing a structural review of the quality of the planning.

Checkpoints:
- Is there a structured process to gather feedback on the budgeting and planning methods used in SOA projects?
- Is there statistic material available on past budgeting and planning schedules for SOA projects?

13.13 Technology and standards

A: Ad hoc technology chosen when needed
Technology and standards for SOA are chosen at the moment a concrete problem arises.

Checkpoints:
- Have basic choices been made with regard to certain SOA technologies and standards?
- Are there SOA standards available within the organization?

B: IT base referential defined and proven
In the field of IT, standards and technologies for SOA have been carefully chosen on the basis of proof of concepts.

Checkpoints:
- Are choices regarding SOA technologies and standards only made when the technology or standard has been tested within the organization in question (via a proof of concept, for example)?
- Has the management of SOA standards been embedded in the organization?

C: Motivated strategy
The choice of standards and technologies issues from a SOA-wide strategy.

Checkpoints:
- Are choices for SOA technologies and standards determined on the basis of the SOA-wide strategy and enterprise architecture of the organization?
- Are choices with regard to SOA technologies and standards made in relation to other technologies and standards?

D: Anticipation of technological changes and new standards adoption
New standards and technologies are continuously followed and implemented as a part of a SOA-wide strategy wherever useful.

Checkpoints:
- Are market developments in the field of SOA technology and standards followed in a proactive way?
- Is there a standard process for the evaluation of new SOA technologies and standards?

13.14 Componentization and reuse

A: Non-coordinated reuse
Reuse and componentization do occur, but that happens more or less by coincidence.

Checkpoints:
- Is there some kind of form of central registration of services that indicates the extent of reuse?
- Are there criteria (such as standards and guidelines) with which a service must comply?

B: Reuse is coordinated within IT (technical services)
Mechanisms have been implemented with IT to force reuse and componentization.

Checkpoints:
- Has a mechanism been implemented to ensure that, when new functionality is required, investigation is carried out to check whether services or components already available can provide this functionality?
- In the field of IT, is there a culture of reusing things before new objects are developed?

C: Reuse is coordinated on the business level (business services)
Mechanisms have been implemented to bring about reuse and componentization on the business level, too.

Checkpoints:
- In the organization, is there a culture of using what there is, before turning to a new process or service?
- In the organization, has a mechanism been implemented to ensure that, at business level, existing processes (steps) and services are reused as much as possible instead?

D: Business and IT are componentized and reuse is common practice
Reuse and componentization is a generally accepted principle in the restructuring of business and IT. It is embedded in the standard working method of the organization with regard to change.

Checkpoints:
- Is there general acceptance within the organization of the culture of first reusing what is available?
- Does the organization have at its disposal a working method for business and IT development in which reuse occupies a prominent position?

13.15 Business processes implementation in the Information System

A: Existing business services within silos

Business services have been implemented in such a way that they are linked to the current silo-like information systems. In this, the links with business processes have not been taken into consideration.

Checkpoints:

- Are business services being designed to make existing systems more open?
- Have the business services been implemented by means of a link to existing systems?

B: Transversal processes

Business services have been implemented, taking into account the links with business processes; one looks beyond the current systems and structures.

Checkpoints:

- Are business services being designed specifically to support business processes?
- Are business services described in terms that are comprehensible and recognizable?
- Are the business processes divided into clearly distinguishable domains?

C: Business Activity Monitoring

Business Activity Monitoring is applied to monitor business processes automatically.

Checkpoints:

- Is use made of Business Activity Monitoring in order to monitor the performance of the business processes?
- Can the performance of the business processes and the business services linked to these, be adequately monitored?

D: Business and IT collaborate to build and deploy business processes

Business and IT collaborate closely to improve the business processes and, using business services that can be linked flexibly, implement these in the organization.

Checkpoints:

- Making use of existing business services, is the business capable of independently implementing new business processes itself?
- Does the organization have at its disposal a standard process by means of which business services are identified, designed, built, and phased out by the business and IT working in mutual cooperation?

13.16 Information System flexibility (infrastructure and applications)

A: Silo-based Information Systems containing service based applications and hardware running them

Information systems are still silos, but use is made of technical services within this type of system.

Checkpoints:

- Has the organization started to open up legacy applications by means of technical services?
- Have technical services been implemented within the organization?

B: Some applications and infrastructure are shared among (hazy) silos due to rationalization

Some application and infrastructural components are made available as services to information systems that still have silo-like features. There is mention of some (technical) reuse.

Checkpoints:

- Have technical services, used more than once, been implemented within the organization?

C: Urbanized, reconfigurable and process-oriented Information System

Information systems now largely consist of business services that are aligned to the business processes that they must support.

Checkpoints:

- Have business services, used more than once, been implemented in the organization?
- Are the functionalities largely made available to the business processes via business services?

D: Decoupled business – information systems virtualization
Information systems are fully disconnected from the business processes they support. Business processes use business services and do not know where and how these are implemented.

Checkpoints:
- Are the business processes in the organization completely disconnected from the systems that support them?
- Can business processes be altered without having to adjust the underlying systems?

13.17 Security

A: Reactive
The organization is aware to a limited extent of the need to protect information. IT has installed a minimum set of security measures. There is a limited awareness of the risks the organization is taking with regard to the protection of messages and services.

Checkpoints:
- Within the organization, is there any awareness of the risks that are being run in the field of information security?
- Has the organization taken any measures to protect messages and services?
- Is information security an issue in the application of SOA?

B: Individual
The organization is more aware of the theme of information security and the risks that are run, but only IT takes any measures, such as the protection of communication through an enterprise service bus. The organization as a whole is not yet genuinely interested in analysing risks and in formulating an information protection policy.

Checkpoints:
- Within the organization, is there widespread awareness of the risks that are being run in the field of information security?
- Has IT taken substantial measures (such as authentication and encryption) to protect messages and services?

C: Collective

There are some enterprise-wide standards and guidelines in the field of information security and the protection of messages and services. Although a start has been made on protecting business processes, there is still a lack of awareness in the business and there is no enterprise-wide information protection policy as yet.

Checkpoints:
- Have enterprise-wide measures been taken to handle the risks in the field of information security?
- Is the business at all aware of the risks that are being run in the field of information security?

D: Proactive

The organization makes use of an enterprise-wide information protection policy that describes all the possible risks and measures with regard to protecting messages and services. Security incidents are analysed and taken into consideration in the elaboration of information protection policy. Business and process managers are responsible for information protection incidents.

Checkpoints:
- Is the organization fully aware of the risks that it is taking in the field of information security?
- Does the organization have at its disposal an enterprise-wide information security policy?
- Is the responsibility for information security embedded in the organization?
- Have measures been taken to protect business processes?

13.18 SOA skills in IT

A: Basic

A basic level of expertise has been built up within IT. IT professionals know about SOA.

Checkpoints:
- Do a substantial number of the IT professionals know about SOA?
- Do a substantial number of the IT professionals have access to the SOA vision and principles of the organization?

B: Moderate

IT professionals have built up a more advanced level of expertise by means of practical application in projects. IT professionals can apply SOA in their work. On average, all IT professionals upon whom SOA has an impact have worked on SOA in one project.

Checkpoints:
* Have a substantial number of IT professionals gained practical experience with SOA?

C: Experienced

IT professionals have built up comprehensive expertise in dealing with SOA. This experience has been gained during several projects. The IT professionals have a mastery of SOA.

Checkpoints:
* Have a substantial number of IT professionals had practical experience with SOA in several projects?
* Have IT professionals given seminar presentations on the way in which the organization deals with SOA?

13.19 SOA skills in Business

A: Basic

A basic level of expertise has been realized. The business professionals know about SOA.

Checkpoints:
* Do a substantial number of the business professionals know about SOA?
* Do a substantial number of the business professionals have access to the SOA vision and principles of the organization?

B: Moderate

Business professionals have built up a following level of expertise by means of practical application in projects. Business professionals can apply SOA in their work. On average, all the business professionals upon whom SOA has an impact have worked on SOA in one project.

Checkpoints:
- Have a substantial number of the business professionals gained practical experience with SOA?

C: Experienced
Business professionals have accumulated comprehensive expertise in dealing with SOA. This experience has been gained in several projects. Business professionals have a mastery of SOA.

Checkpoints:
- Have a substantial number of the business professionals acquired practical experience with SOA in several projects?
- Have the business professionals given seminar presentations about how the organization deals with SOA?

13.20 SOA mindset and knowledge among IT People

A: Sparse awareness
There is sporadic knowledge of SOA within the IT organization. Many people have heard the term, but they cannot place it and certainly cannot indicate what the advantages for the organization might be.

Checkpoints:
- Does the majority of the IT organization have any knowledge of SOA?

B: Organization-level awareness
Within the IT organization there is broad awareness of what SOA is and what the advantages might be for the business organization. However, there is also a prevalence of scepticism and resistance against the consequences that the implementation of SOA entails.

Checkpoints:
- Does the majority of the IT organization recognize the advantages of SOA for their own organization?
- Does the majority of the IT organization have a comprehensive knowledge of SOA?

C: Common SOA mindset

SOA enjoys broad support in the IT organization. The advantages and consequences of the implementation are clear and generally accepted. The IT organization is impatient to reap the advantages of SOA.

Checkpoints:
- Does the majority of the IT organization know what the consequences of implementing SOA will be for their own organization?
- Is there a broad support base for the implementation of SOA within the IT organization?

13.21 SOA mindset and knowledge among Business People

A: Sparse awareness

There is sporadic knowledge of SOA within the business organization. Many people have heard the term, but they cannot place it and certainly cannot indicate what the advantages for the organization might be.

Checkpoints:
- Does the majority of the business organization have any knowledge of SOA?

B: Organization-level awareness

Within the business organization there is broad awareness of what SOA is and what the advantages might be for the business organization. However, there is also a prevalence of scepticism and resistance against the consequences that the implementation of SOA entails.

Checkpoints:
- Does the majority of the business organization recognize the advantages of SOA for their own organization?
- Does the majority of the business organization have a comprehensive knowledge of SOA?

C: Common SOA mindset

SOA is widely supported in the business organization. The advantages and consequences of the implementation are clear and generally accepted. The business organization is impatient to reap the advantages of SOA.

Checkpoints:
- Does the majority of the business organization recognize the consequences of implementing SOA for their own organization?
- Is there a broad support base for the implementation of SOA within the business organization?

13.22 To conclude

The employment of SOA involves many factors. In this Appendix, we have defined 20 of them – each one with its own developmental path. That is too many for an organization to address all at once. The SOA Maturity Model is an instrument to focus attention on specific areas, one at a time. Using the checkpoints to focus more narrowly on development in each area, it is possible to determine the status of an organization. Mapping the organization on the Maturity Model can identify the key areas that need to be emphasized in the near future and can clarify the extent to which this should be done.

References

Acharya, Amit et al., *SOA Foundation Service Creation Scenario*, IBM Redbook, 2006, http://publib-b.boulder.ibm.com/Redbooks.nsf/RedpieceAbstracts/sg247240.html?Open

Ang, Jenny et al., *SOA antipaFterns*, 2005, http://www-128.ibm.com/developerworks/webservices/library/ws-antipatterns/

Arsanjani, Ali et al., *The SOA solution stack, an architectural reference model*, 2005

Bartlett, Christopher and Sumantra Ghoshal, *Managing Across Boarders – the transnational solution*, Harvard Business School Press, 2002

Belbin, Meredith, *Management Teams*, Oxford, 2004

Berg, Martin van den and Marlies van Steenbergen, *Building an Enterprise Architecture Practice*, Springer, 2006a

Berg, Martin van den and Erik van Ommeren, *Verbied services! De verplichte relatie tussen EA en SOA*, Informatie, October 2006b

Bieberstein, Norbert, *Human Services Bus Stays Human* at http://soaprojectmanager.com, December 22, 2006.

Bieberstein, Norbert et al., *Impact of Service Oriented Architecture on enterprise systems, organizational structures, and individuals*, IBM Systems Journal 44-4, 2005a, http://www.research.ibm.com/journal/sj/444/bieberstein.html

Bieberstein, Norbert et al., *Service Oriented Architecture Compass: Business Value, Planning and Enterprise Roadmap*, Prentice-Hall, 2005b

Bieberstein, Norbert et al., *Transformational Impact of SOA on Corporations – Challenges to IT Systems, Organization Structures and Individuals*, IBM Systems Journal, Vol. 44-4, 2005c

Bloem, Jaap et al., *Making IT Governance Work in a Sarbanes-Oxley World*, Wiley, 2005

Bloomberg, Jason, *When Not to Use an SOA*, Zapflash-02162004, 2004, www.zapthink.com

Broadbent, Marianne and Peter Weill, *Leading Governance Business and IT Processes*, ITEP Findings, 2002

Brown, Carol and Jeanne W. Ross, *The IT Organization of the 21st Century: Moving to a Process-Based Orientation*, CISR WP No. 306, MIT Sloan, 1999, http://web.mit.edu/cisr/working%20papers/cisrwp306.pdf.

Buckingham, Marcus, *Now, Discover your Strengths*, The Free Press, 2001

CBDi Journal, *SOA Fundamentals*, 2005, http://www.cbdiforum.com/

CIO Asia, *The Truth about SOA*, 2006, http://cioasia.com/ShowPage.aspx?pagetype=2&articleid=4021&pubid=5&issueid=98

CIO Insight, *Case Study: Starwood Hotels Uses SOA to Improve Guest Services and Cut Costs*, 2006, http://www.cioinsight.com/article2/0,1397,1954594,00.asp

Colan, Mark, *Five entry points*, 2006, http://www.xmlone.org/xmlasia2006/slides/ibm-colon-5-entry-points-for-soa.pdf

DiMare, Jay et al., *The business Value of SOA*, IBM Institute for Business Value, 2006, www.ibm.com

Dueck, Gunther, *Wild Duck, Empirische Philosophie der Mensch-Computer-Vernetzung*, Markus Kaminski, 2005

Friedman, Thomas, *The World Is Flat*, Allen Lane, 2005

Galbraith, Jay R., *Designing the Global Corporation*, Jossey-Bass, 2000

Gartner, *Introduction to Service Oriented Architecture*, Gartner Research ID-number SPA-19-5971, 2003

Gartner, *A Portal May Be Your First Step to Leverage SOA*, Gartner Research ID-number G00130149, 2006a

Gartner, *Maximize Your SOA Investment via Policy Enforcement*, Gartner Research ID-number G00141010, 2006b

Gartner, *Sample Governance Mechanisms for a Service Oriented Architecture*, Gartner Research ID-number G00139465, 2006c

Gartner, *Service Oriented Architectures Craves Governance*, Gartner Research ID-number G00135396, 2006d

Gartner, SOA: *Where do I Start?*, Gartner Research ID-number G00130149, 2006e

Ghoshal, Sumantra and Christopher Bartlett, *The Individualized Corporation*, Harper Business Books, 1999

Heffner, Randy, *Survey Data Says: The Time For SOA Is Now*, Forrester Research, 2006

Herrington, Jack, *Cook up your own with these recipes*, 2006, http://www-128.ibm.com/developerworks/opensource/library/os-php-dhtml1/

High, Rob, Stephen Kinder, Steve Graham, *IBM's SOA foundation*, 2005, http://download.boulder.ibm.com/ibmdl/pub/software/dw/webservices/ws-soa-whitepaper.pdf

Hoogervorst, Jan, *Enterprise Governance & Architectuur*, SDU, 2006

IBM, *Collaborations and communications, On Demand Workplace*, 2005a, http://www.ibm.com/ibm/responsibility/people/communications/ondemand-workplace.shtml

IBM, *IBM SOA Foundation, Providing what you need to get started with* SOA, 2005b,

IBM, *Entry Points into SOA*, 2006a, http://akamai.infoworld.com/spotlights/soa/SOA_Entry_Points.pdf

IBM, *SOA From A Business Centric Perspective*, 2006b, http://www.infoworld.com/event/soa/docs/IE_051606_Sandy_CARTER_IBM_Websphere_Marketing.ppt

IBM, *SOA Governance*, 2006c, http://www306.ibm.com/software/solutions/soa/gov/

IBM Global Business Services, *Component business models, Making specialization real*, 2005, www.ibm.com

IBM Global Business Services, *Expanding the Innovation Horizon, the Global CEO Study 2006*, 2006a, www.ibm.com

IBM Global Business Services, *Service Oriented Architecture, a practical guide to measuring return on that investment*, 2006b, www.ibm.com

IFAC, *Enterprise Governance, Getting the Balance Right*, 2004, www.ifac.org

IT Governance Institute, *Board Briefing on IT Governance*, 2003, www.itgi.org

Kaplan, Robert and David Norton, *Strategy Maps*, Harvard Business School Press, 2004

Koomen, Tim et al., *TMap Next, for result-driven testing*, Tutein Nolthenius, 2006

Macehitter, Neil and Neil Ward-Dutton, *On IT-business alignment*, 2005, www.mwdadvisors.com

Macehitter, Neil and Neil Ward-Dutton, *Service Oriented Architecture: handle with care*, 2005, www.mwdadvisors.com

O'Reilly, Tim, *What is Web 2.0*, 2005, http://www.oreillynet.com/pub/a/oreilly/tim/news/2005/09/30/what-is-web-20.html

Rogue Wave, White Paper, *The business case for SOA*, 2006, www.roguewave.com

Smit, Gerard, et al., *Face-to-face, SOE and what are you doing with SOA*, 2006 http://www.nl.capgemini.com/m/nl/f2f/service_oriented_enterprise/02_Alliances.pdf

Smits, Daniel, *Succes met IT Governance*, Sogeti, 2006

Wagter, Roel et al., *Dynamic Enterprise Architecture, How to Make It Work*, Wiley, 2005

Weblayers, *Policy Based Governance for the Enterprise*, White paper, 2005a, www.weblayers,com

Weblayers, SOA *Governance, Introduction*, White paper, 2005b, www.weblayers.com

Weill, Peter and Jeanne W. Ross, *IT Governance: How Top Performers Manage IT Decision Rights for Superior Results*, Harvard Business Press, 2004

Wikipedia, www.wikipedia.org

Index

About IBM

At IBM, we strive to lead in the invention, development and manufacture of the industry's most advanced information technologies, including computer systems, software, storage systems and microelectronics. We translate these advanced technologies into value for our customers through our professional solutions, services and consulting businesses worldwide. IBM is aligned around a single, focused business model: innovation. IBM takes its breadth and depth of insight on issues, processes and operations across a variety of industries, and invents and applies technology to help solve its clients' most intractable business and competitive problems. Although we remain committed, as ever, to lead the development of state-of-the-art technologies, and the products and service offerings built around them, we measure ourselves today by how well we help clients solve their biggest and most pressing problems.

About Sogeti

Sogeti, a leader in IT services and proximity engineering, offers a range of local professional services in Information Technology and High-Tech Consulting for large companies through these three complementary areas:

- Application Services, or systems integration.
  From conception to maintenance of information systems: consulting, architecture, support, development, integration, testing and maintenance of application assets.
- Infrastructure Services, or integration management and systems administration.
  From the integration of technical infrastructures to the implementation of IT systems: consulting, technical architecture, engineering, integration, installation and administration of systems and networks, implementation management and user support.
- High Tech, or High-Tech Consulting.
  Outsourcing Research and Development, and Innovation Advice. Scientific and technical research and development, mechanical design, development of complex systems.

Sogeti employs more than 18,000 professionals in France, Belgium, Denmark, Luxembourg, Ireland, Germany, Netherlands, Spain, Switzerland, Sweden, the United Kingdom and the United States.

For more information, go to: www.sogeti.com

About the authors

Martin van den Berg

Martin van den Berg is the Architecture Service Line Manager at Sogeti Nederland B.V. In this role he is responsible for the development of architectural services and expertise in Sogeti. Additionally he provides guidance to organizations in the professionalization of Enterprise Architecture and the implementation of Service Oriented Architecture. He is one of the founders of DYA and co-author of *Dynamic Enterprise Architecture, How to make it work* and *Building an Enterprise Architecture Practice*. Martin van den Berg is also chairman of the architecture section of the Dutch Computer Society. Martin has published several articles and is a much sought after speaker at architecture seminars.

Martin.vanden.Berg@sogeti.nl

Norbert Bieberstein

Norbert Bieberstein works for IBM's SOA Advanced Technologies organization and is responsible for the worldwide publication and communication of SOA related topics. He gained first-hand experiences from customer projects, in various industries, striving to migrate to SOA based solutions. Norbert published several articles on SOA-related topics, coordinated the IBM Systems Journal issue 44-4 on SOA, and was the lead author of *Service Oriented Architecture Compass* (ISBN 0-13-187002-5). Before he co-authored two IBM's redBooks *Introduction to Grid Computing with Globus* (SG24-6895-01) and *Enabling Applications for Grid Computing with Globus* (SG24-6936-00), and published the book *CASE Tools* (ISBN: 3446175261). He entered IBM as a software engineering consultant at the software development labs in 1989. In total he has over 27 years of experience in Information Technology and Computer Sciences. Before IBM he worked as an application developer at a smaller software vendor and as a scientific programmer at Aachen University of Technology (RWTH), where he also received his masters in Mathematics and Geography. Recently, he completed a corporate MBA program at Henley Management College in the UK.

bsn@de.ibm.com

Per Björkegren

Per Björkegren is one of the leading Enterprise Architects and IT strategists in Sweden. He is the practice leader for Architecture and IT Governance within Sogeti Sweden, developing the service offerings and speaking at open seminars. Per is the founder and president of SWEAN (Swedish Enterprise Architecture Network), which currently has about 350 members. Per spends most of his time 'out in the bush' supporting many large organizations in Sweden regarding IT driven business development, enterprise architecture and IT management. Per has a broad background in IT, ranging from software development to architecture and business management via an extensive set of service offering development assignments on global Capgemini level.

Per.Bjorkegren@sogeti.se

Jean-Marc Gaultier

Jean-Marc Gaultier is the Vice-President in charge of the alliance with IBM for the Sogeti Group. He has a broad international sales background in IT with sales management experience, ranging from Software control testing to Local Professional Services and Outsourcing, in Europe and the US. In his current role, Jean-Marc helps the Sogeti Group increase its offering, skills and sales around the IBM technology.

jean-marc.gaultier@sogeti.com

Lon L. Holden

Lon is a Worldwide Solutions Manager within IBM Software Group. In this role Lon is responsible for working with system integrators to most effectively leverage IBM technology within their solution offerings. The focus is on determining where the use of technology will provide significant added value to clients, while also providing competitive differentiation in the integrator's offerings. Lon has a broad background in the IT consulting industry including software development, methodology, and project management. Lon specializes in understanding and applying technology in a business context.

lholden@us.ibm.com

Manuel de Juan

Manuel de Juan is the Technical Manager and member of the IT Innovation Office at Sogeti Spain. Since his start with IT he has devoted his professional efforts to solving integration issues between systems, either as a software developer, analyst or project manager. When asked about his political preferences, he always says: 'I'm in the middleware'.

manuel.dejuan@sogeti.com

Tim Koomen

Tim Koomen is Manager and Strategist of the Testing R&D team at Sogeti Netherlands B.V., covering issues like testing in agile environments (DSDM, RUP), Test Process Improvement, testing in SOA and test strategies. He is the co-author of the TPI book, published in Dutch, English, German and Japanese, co-editor of the TMap Test Topics book, published in Dutch and English, co-author of TMap Next (Dutch, English and German (soon)) and frequently speaks at conferences (Eurostar '97-'06, ICSTest (4x), Quality Week Europe '99, SQE Congress 2000, Quality Week 2000, Conquest 2001, StarEast 2003) and training sessions throughout Europe and the United States. In 2003 he received the European Testing Excellence Award for his work on TPI, TMap and testing in general.

Tim.Koomen@sogeti.nl

Craig Mayer

Craig Mayer is a Director at Sogeti USA, with over twenty-five years of domestic and international executive level experience in management, information technology, and operations in a diversity of industries. His primary expertise lies in the alignment of business and information technology strategy, with additional deep expertise in business reorganization and re-engineering. In addition to Service Oriented Architecture experience and skills going back to the late 1990s, he also has expertise in business process integration and effectiveness, Sarbanes-Oxley – CobIT – ITIL assessment and compliance, kaizen and gemba kaizen (continuous improvement), and risk-based/quality-centric software testing. Craig holds a Ph.D. (ABD) in Anthropology from Southern Methodist University (Dallas, Texas).

Craig.Mayer@us.sogeti.com

Erik van Ommeren

Erik van Ommeren is a Business Development Manager at Sogeti Nederland B.V. He is one of the initiators of the Service Oriented Architecture initiatives at Sogeti in the Netherlands. Erik has a broad background in IT with experience ranging from software development using many different technologies, to architecture and management. In his current role he is responsible for developing new service offerings for Sogeti. Part of his time is spent advising organizations on architectural decisions, transformation projects and innovation. Erik is also a trainer, speaker at seminars and author of several articles.

Erik.van.Ommeren@sogeti.nl

Philippe Ravix

Philippe Ravix is an IS architect and SOA Service Line Manager at Sogeti France. He is responsible for the development of architecture services at Sogeti. He advises organizations on architectural decisions and counsels several majors companies in their transformation projects. Philippe is also a trainer, speaker at SOA events and author of white papers.

philippe.ravix@sogeti.com

Bruno Rizzi

Bruno Rizzi is the SOA Leader at Sogeti AS France for the Industry and Telecommunications Divisions. He is one of the creators of the Sogeti SOA offering in France. He has extensive experience in IT including software development, qualimetry, project management and architecture and has worked as JEE expert for several major French companies. Bruno now shares his time between the business development of the SOA offering and architecture counseling for Sogeti's clients.

bruno.rizzi@sogeti.fr